DARE TO BE YOU
WHAT OTHERS ARE SAYING ABOUT *DARE TO BE YOU* . . .

Dare to be You "discusses the concept of being and growing, and in coffee-break language. Dolby so well knows what he is talking about that he can talk plainly. . . . For its practical explanations of conscience, and for its understanding and loving exploration of Man, Dolby's book is bound to be much appreciated, widely read, and often quoted."
Sherman R. Hanson, *Christian Literature Commission*

"Here is a fresh breeze in books on the Christian and modern psychology. Dr. Dolby . . . writes a book that leads the reader through many current topics in a clear and interesting manner. It can also be an adventure in self-discovery."
The Baptist Herald

"Dr. Dolby illustrates how psychology contributes to a better understanding and appreciation of the Christian personality. . . . This is a good book."
The Reformed Journal

[The section entitled "As the Twig Is Bent" traces] ". . . the spiritual and emotional development of a child from birth through the college years. I cannot recall reading a better profile. Readable, concise, and rich in suggestions, these chapters should be most helpful to parents and teachers. I found this book probing, enlightening, and reassuring."
The Church Herald

"Dr. Dolby has succeeded in placing another piece in the bridge from traditionalism to knowledgeable, insightful Christian commitment. . . . [He] has accomplished a rare achievement in combining biblical theology with professional psychology. This integration has been accomplished, because it is admittedly the story of the author's own struggles and personal insights into the Christian life both as a man, and as a practicing professional in the field of clinical psychology as well."

Dr. Richard H. Cox, *Eternity*

"This is an exciting mind-stretching book—especially for those who are involved in a counseling ministry. . . . the 'mind-stretching quality' is demonstrated in the author's ability to communicate simply and clearly some profound concepts."

Bibliotheca Sacra

"Great, refreshing, stimulating and thought-provoking are some of my feelings concerning this book. [It] could well be used for discussion groups."

Standard Publishing

"This excellent book . . . is must reading."

Evangelical Beacon

"This book is a lively, freshly written approach toward bridging the gap between those involved in the investigation of human behavior and those committed to a Christian view of the understanding of man. . . . Written for laymen. . . . *Dare to Be You* [is] a stimulating, honest and valuable presentation of the issues that Christians need to squarely face."

Provident Book Finder

DARE TO BE YOU

A
Psychologist's
Reflections
on
Christian
Experience

James R. Dolby

(original title: I, Too, Am Man)

A Key-Word Book
WORD BOOKS, Publisher
Waco, Texas

A KEY-WORD BOOK
Published by Pillar Books for Word Books, Publisher.

DARE TO BE YOU

Formerly published as *I, Too, Am Man.*
Copyright © 1969 by Word Incorporated, Waco, Texas. All rights reserved. No part of this book may be reproduced in any form, except for brief quotations in reviews, without the written permission of the publisher.

Library of Congress catalog card number: 69–12815
ISBN #0–87680–872–0
Printed in the United States of America
First Key-Word Book edition July 1976

Some of the chapters of this book appeared in slightly different form as articles in various magazines. "I, Too, Am Man" and "Yes! But to What?" appeared in *Eternity;* "Guilt" was published in June, 1968, *Christian Herald* as "Christianity and Guilt"; "Spiritual Guidance" appeared in the April, 1969, *Christian Herald;* "Giving" was published in *Christian Life,* December, 1968, as "The Human Need to Give." Other chapters ran in the *Journal of the American Scientific Affiliation,* and the *Wheaton College Faculty Bulletin.*

TO
Jan
a gracious friend and
loving wife, whose help
and encouragement made
this book possible

CONTENTS

INTRODUCTION

As a clinical psychologist I have often been frustrated and disappointed when Christians could not accept or assimilate the insights which the psychologists or other social scientists had to offer. Any new way of discussing man was frequently rejected as a threat to religious orthodoxy. The "old" ways of talking about man appeared to be synonymous with truth, especially if they contained some Biblical phrases. Discussing a religious experience from a psychological point of view seemed to indicate to some people that one was trying to explain away the experience or eliminate any "spiritual" quality in it.

Because I sensed some of the average Christian's fear, and because I was often frustrated in my attempts to shed new light on an issue, I purposed to help educate the knowledgeable Christian layman. I began by writing a number of articles which were accepted for publication in Christian periodicals. Then I began to think of collecting them in book form. This book is the result.

Dare to Be You is not written for the professional psychologist, mental health worker, or trained social scientist, although they may find it interesting. It is written for the layman who is interested and willing to think new thoughts and to begin bridging the gap between those involved in the investigation of human behavior and those committed to a Christian world view. The book has not been written to answer questions; it is meant to be a springboard for discussion regarding the various areas of religious experience. If sections of this book produce anxiety and precipitate good dialogue, it will have been of value from my point of view.

I am personally committed to an orthodox Christian perspective. Therefore one of my intentions has been to help the layman organize his thoughts so that he will be able to communicate the Christian message to the present generation. The insights of the social scientists must be given high priority in any discussion which is relevant to the needs of man today. My experiences with college students have been of great value because their questions often forced me to rethink—and to integrate if possible—some of my thoughts as a human being with my experiences as a clinical psychologist into a meaningful statement on various religious issues.

Commitment to Jesus the Christ in this era is accompanied by many intellectual and emotional struggles. This book is in part a record of some of my personal frustrations as a Christian in a sophisticated, knowledgeable, and "mod" culture. It is my hope that a record of some of these struggles may be of help to others who are trying to be Christian in an informed post-Christian era.

I am convinced that new ideas are not a major threat to a person who has an inquiring mind, a stable personality structure, and who is willing to accept his finiteness. New perspectives will cause anxiety in some, especially those with a highly crystallized faith. But the danger of stagnation and irrelevance is a great threat to all Christianity, and to combat it we must seek to engage the minds of our generation. I hope that this book will be helpful to those who are honestly searching for faith in the twentieth century.

DARE TO BE YOU

To tell another person of one's own failure, guilt, insecurities, lust, and love may be as difficult a task as a person will ever have in his entire lifetime. It has been said that some people would rather die than be known.

I, TOO, AM MAN

You and I are basically dishonest. Most of our lives have been spent learning to play the game of deception; we have been tutored long and well. In our attempts to conceal who we really are from our friends and loved ones, we find that we have betrayed ourselves. Too often we ourselves believe the lies which we are trying to get others to accept. Once in a while we want to stop playing this game of make-believe, but when we try to stop we are confronted with the depressing and startling truth. We cannot stop. When we ask ourselves the question, "Who am I?" we don't know; and we find that no matter how hard we struggle, we are not able to find out. We are caught in a pattern of dishonesty . . . to be honest with ourselves is not natural.

What do I mean when I say that we are deceiving ourselves and really do not know who we are? Most people live with assumptions about themselves which have never been tested, and the behavior patterns resulting from these assumptions also go unchallenged. We have spent most of our lives learning from peers, adults, and parents, especially parents, what roles to play and what they think of us. We frequently assume that if this is their view of us, it is correct—but is this an adequate assumption? Perhaps what they have been telling us about ourselves for these years is inaccurate.

What do *you* think of yourself? Are you intellectually bright, dull, or just average? Are you pretty, ugly, or plain? Are you an introvert or extrovert; neither or both? Are you selfish or unselfish; good or bad, or both? All of these views of yourself are in large measure learned from signifi-selfish or unselfish; good or bad, or both? All of these assumptions present an accurate picture of yourself?

We want to be accepted and loved; and we know that to gain such acceptance we must play the roles imposed upon us by our subculture—the people and circumstances around us. We also hide truths about ourselves which do not agree with the expectations of the significant people in our world. The assumption is that if these people knew what we were really like they would reject us and place us outside the circle of their love. Paul Tournier says: "What isolates the patient the most in his life—whether schoolboy, housewife, or worker,—is the very thing that isolates us the most: our secrets." [1] One school of psychotherapy says that mental illness is the byproduct of estrangement from one-self—the result of chronic self-deception.

In a desperate attempt to be loved, we have betrayed ourselves and lost our identity. We are trying with all that is within us to preserve what little love we have been able to obtain. We have played the role of the pious one, the buffoon, the scholar, the dunce, the self-contained, the athlete, the iconoclast, the beauty, the professor, the lover, the intellectual, the saint, the leader; but if we were asked who we really were, we probably could not say. It is possible that the self-contained is really insecure, the intellectual afraid of his emotions, the iconoclast full of hate, the saint full of sin, the lover basically insecure in his sex role, the buffoon really sensitive, the beauty lonely.

Two great questions of life are "Who am I?" and "How can I find out who I am?" Because we have played the roles given us by our subculture, and because we are afraid to tell truths about ourselves for fear of personal rejection

---

[1] *Escape from Loneliness*, p. 44.

and loss of love, we find the task of self-discovery very difficult—and sometimes impossible. I often find it hard to be myself. I am pressed to play many roles: professor, counselor, husband, a special kind of Christian, professional psychologist. Each role carries with it different, though many times overlapping, behavior patterns. If I try to break through the superficial social expectations of each role, I will be met with opposition from without and within.

The pressures from without may be fatal, they may destroy the possibility of self-discovery or personal honesty. They may press in till one gasps for air and pleads for mercy. I can hear the voices of the pressures from without—"Have you changed?" "We don't understand you." "You had better be more careful." "Don't be naïve." "How could you say that and be truly Christian?" "He must be having difficulties in his spiritual life." Often at this point people give up the task of self-discovery. These pressures are too great. We find ourselves inadequate to break through the walls of protection and provincialism. We have lost ourselves in all our complexity.

The pressures from within assault our integrity, and we try to resist change and self-awareness. These inner voices say: "The older and wiser say it is true—don't challenge it." "My parents might reject me if I change; can I stand to be rejected by those from whom I need love most?" "If I open the door I may not be able to stop uninvited guests." "I might really be motivated by hate and condescension rather than love." "What if I find my Christian service is a product of fear rather than concern for Christ and His Kingdom?" "What if I find the formulas given for the Christian life really don't work?" "Can I live with the insecurity of unanswered questions?" "What if my views of truth are just defenses and mere products of my personality?" "What if I find out I'm not loved and accepted for who I am but because I'm what other people want me to be?" To be honest about ourselves, we must resist these inner voices.

Once in a while we may get a glimmer of what lies behind the façade. The real person emerges: perhaps shy, insecure, hostile, sensitive, lonely, sinful, and perhaps capable of great virtue. When we have tried to express these brief insights we may have been met with lack of understanding

15

and an appeal to "be yourself." When we begin to express ourselves honestly, occasionally we are made the object of prayer, considered a "backslider," or even rejected by well-meaning Christians. The tragic thing is that these people, too, have been caught in the web of dishonesty and are unable to find their way out. The door of self-analysis which was once open to them has been closed and tightly sealed by chronic self-deception.

Personal dishonesty is an insidious disease. Once begun, it slowly destroys the person until he is no longer aware that he has betrayed himself. And still the cancer continues to eat away at the core of life, the real self. It eats away until a man can become unaware of basic truths about himself. An example of this is the person who comes before a Christian congregation and talks about "victory in the Christian life," "loving one another," and "God in you." He can smile, shake hands after the service, and leave the holy sanctuary with lust, fear, pride, and idolatry within him. The tragedy is, *he may not ever know it was there.*

Perhaps this is too dark a picture, but I have seen many persons in psychotherapy who have had a great deal of difficulty shedding the many layers of self-deception to eventually find the true self. It is a hard job! To tell another person of one's failure, guilt, insecurities, lust, and love may be as difficult a task as a person will ever have in his entire lifetime. It has been said that some people would rather die than be known.

We can find out who we are *only* in the presence of one we can trust and respect. Jourard, a psychologist from the University of Florida, says, ". . . it seems to be another empirical fact that no man can come to know himself except as an outcome of disclosing himself to another person." [2] The reason that I as a psychologist can listen and at times understand is that I too am made of the same stuff and am painfully and joyously aware of it—I too am man.

Your friends and acquaintances are like you, with similar problems, inhibitions, fears, and desires. Why can't we share our humanness and learn to love each other for who we are? We can't because we are afraid of being betrayed

[2] *The Transparent Self,* p. 5.

16

and losing love. It was Dietrich Bonhoeffer who said, "Many Christians are unthinkably horrified when a real sinner is discovered among the righteous. So we remain alone in our sin, living in lies and hypocrisy." [3]

What a tragic but true statement about the Church, God's Church—a tragedy of dishonesty! Hobart Mowrer, a well-known psychologist, has said: "One would think that the church would be the place where people could confront one another openly and honestly, since the Church historically has made no pretense about man's condition and his need of redemption. But all too often the Church is today a place where people hide behind Biblicism, and dogma, and theology." [4]

What this world is looking for is men and women who are honest with themselves, with life, and with God—men who are not afraid to be themselves. J. D. Salinger, through his dramatic portrayal of Holden Caulfield in the book, *Catcher in the Rye,* places an epitaph across twentieth-century America, and perhaps across mankind in general. It reads: MAN IS A PHONY. If there is any group of people that cannot afford the luxury of having that epitaph inscribed over them, it is the Christian church. How tragic to wake up one morning finding the church doors closed and a sign on the door reading: "You don't understand yourselves or us; therefore we have no need of you. Signed, *The World.*"

Self-knowledge affects all areas of Christian experience. If we do not know who we are, what kind of a prayer life can we lead? What can we pray for? How can we pray for ourselves and others if we do not know them or ourselves? All we can say is, "God, try me, and search me. Help me to find out about myself so that I can understand and help other people." We should ask God in moments of quietness before him to help us see ourselves. We should spend times of meditation in his Word asking for self-perception. We must admit doubts, failure—be truly ourselves before him.

How can we go further about the business of knowing ourselves? We can do this by being as honest as we can

[3] *Life Together,* p. 110.
[4] *The New Group Therapy,* pp. 72–73.

with at least one trusted person to whom we can confess our shortcomings, tell about our joys, our doubts, our feelings, and all our deep thoughts. Honesty is contagious. Once we begin to be honest with ourselves and with others, it becomes easier. Then we find that we can be honest with an ever-increasing number of persons.

Perhaps one of our main tasks will be to try to understand others—forget about advice giving and listen. Try to understand when others are being honest with us. Listen to their confessions and their innermost secrets with a deep sense of appreciation and respect because they are giving us the greatest gift that can be given—part of themselves.

We never will be able to apprehend completely the illusive "true self," but we can make strides in that direction. At times we will bog down in morbid introspection; on other occasions we will allow a great personal insight to slip through our fingers as if it were irrelevant. The journey of self-discovery will be lifelong; the moments of rejection and despondency will be many; but there will be illuminating moments and days of rich personal satisfaction to the person who attempts to be honest with himself and with his God.

BIBLIOGRAPHY

Bonhoeffer, Dietrich. *Life Together*. New York: Harper & Row, Inc., 1954.

Jourard, Sidney M. *The Transparent Self*. Princeton: D. Van Nostrand Co., Inc., 1964.

Mowrer, O. Hobart. *The New Group Therapy*. Princeton: D. Van Nostrand Co., Inc., 1964.

Tournier, Paul. *Escape from Loneliness*. Philadelphia: The Westminster Press, 1962.

GIVING

When we give of ourselves we become vulnerable, and we may be hurt. . . . Giving ourselves in marriage or in commitment to any cause may be frightening; and some of us would rather give money and let the others get on the firing line.

2

GIVING

A Twisted Ashtray and a Good-night Hug

I was talking to a competent young secretary the other day who had recently decided to continue with her present employer after turning down a lucrative offer at another place. Her explanation of the decision was that she believed that loyalty to her present employer was the real factor in the decision. This is an admirable motive and highly commendable.

As we pursued the topic further, however, it came out that there were several factors besides loyalty that influenced her decision. She was a little apprehensive about establishing a whole new set of relationships, she would not have such a prestigious position, and to top it off, she would have to begin the day earlier and would have less free time. Under the explanation of "loyalty" were a number of less lofty but nonetheless real and personally meaningful motives.

It is difficult for any of us to accept the idea that our motives for doing anything are not as simple and praiseworthy as we like to think they are. As a matter of fact, our motives are always complex and often unconscious.

Acknowledging this fact and then examining our motives is a step in the direction of the personal honesty required of all Christians.

Take the matter of Christian giving. If we will examine the motivation that prompts a great deal of giving to Christian causes, we will find, combined with the desire to give to the work of Christ, a number of other human motives. These are often unclear and unstated but are very important.

As I came home one evening, my spirits were lifted to see the children in the neighborhood enthusiastically gathered around one child who usually was left out. She was a shy, quiet, frightened little girl who spent a great deal of time dreaming and hoping that the girls in the block would invite her out to play with them. I was most curious as to why she had suddenly become so popular. As I edged over to the group to see what was going on, the first thing I saw was that all of the children were attentively eating popsicles which apparently had been given them by this girl. It became painfully obvious to me that she was accepted, at least for the present, because she had tried to build a bridge to their friendship with a gift.

The experiences of our youth become part of our complex, influential past, and they often erupt into the present and frustrate our highest motives. The pattern of giving in youth can become a pattern for a lifetime. Like the little girl, many of us give to the church unconsciously hoping that by giving to God we will receive, either from God or from the church, acceptance and love in return. We give in order to get.

This barter form of giving becomes especially necessary when a person is deprived of affection from parents or peers in the growing-up process. The sensitive human being weeps internally when he sees a child who has to offer a fistful of candy to be accepted by his peers. The same sensitivity should be shown to the adult who gives to Christian programs with the haunting youthful hope that in so doing he will find love and acceptance by God. This is the way it was done in childhood and the unconscious fantasies of youth still linger.

It is likely that one of the major reasons for giving is to avoid guilt feelings. This is true especially of a Christian

22

perspective that is very authoritative and that tends to define appropriate religious behavior rather precisely. For many, the tithe, 10 percent of one's earnings, has become part of this precise religious piety. It makes no difference if it is 10 percent from a family in poverty earning three thousand dollars a year or 10 percent of a twenty-thousand-dollar income. The important point is not what is left over to live with, but the 10 percent.

Many a man has hovered over his checkbook worrying about what the "Father" in heaven would do if he gave only 7 percent of his income this year, especially if it was considered after taxes had been deducted. One can mentally picture the same man hovering over his income tax wondering if the government will review his income tax return and if they will catch some of the "slight" exaggerations. This man's God is probably made in the image of his father who was there to punish him for the little fib, or for taking a few extra pieces of candy out of the jar. Many a man out of guilt feelings has rewritten the check for fear of God's judgment. Persons like this give rather generously, but they receive as much joy out of giving as they do paying their yearly income tax.

What we think about God is very much related to how and why we give. It is well documented that our concept of God is often close to what we think of our fathers. (More will be said about this later.) This God-Father connection is also reinforced by such prayers as the Lord's Prayer which begins, "Our Father who art in heaven . . ." If we believe that God is punitive, strict, and judgmental, we will have great hesitancy about cheating him out of what we believe he requires. An "eye for an eye and a tooth for a tooth" concept of God will cause the strongest of persons to quake under the potential wrath of an all-knowing God. Ten percent of one's earnings is nothing compared to God's judgment, so the argument goes.

Other people have grown up with different kinds of fathers. Some were fortunate enough to have a father who consistently showed affection and could forgive readily. This type of father is easy to love and accept. Even though the father may have had to be firm, the child knows that he is loved no matter what the difficulty is. Giving to a God conceived of in this image will be different. Instead of mechanical giving motivated by fear, we will be more likely to give as a result of genuine affection and because God is thought of as longsuffering and gracious with rebellious, mischievous children.

The person weighted down with a burden of guilt is a depressed, unhappy, rejected creature; from a professional perspective he is a candidate for mental illness. The fact that some people relieve their guilt feelings through forms of penance is obvious. This penance may take the form of church work, involvement in social reforms, hours of prayer, or even self-punishment. Everybody does penance in his own way. It is speculated that many, if not most, accidents are the result of unconscious needs to pay for sins committed which have gone unpunished. Some persons suffer from migraine headaches and other psychosomatic illnesses as a form of self-punishment to relieve guilt feelings.

For many, the giving of money, effort, or time to Christian work is an attempt to do penance. It is a way of paying for the errors done and is therapeutic from a psychological point of view. O. H. Mowrer, a psychologist of repute, hypothesizes that the reason psychotherapy is effective is due to the fact that it costs so much that the person going through this procedure literally "pays for" the wrongdoings which caused the neurosis in the first place. Although this is not a widely accepted hypothesis in the mental health profession, it does point out the possible relationship between the giving of money and penance.

Many of us have substituted the giving of money for the giving of ourselves. Young people are rebelling against the materialistic society which offers money and things but not deep interpersonal relationships and love. This is often true in the church. We can give money to a church or a cause without giving ourselves either in work or in interest. The money becomes a way of having a form of religious piety without personally becoming involved. In his book *The Meaning of Gifts*, Tournier makes the point often that "the supreme gift is the giving of oneself." The gift of money can be a way of bypassing this form of personal commitment.

When we give of ourselves we become vulnerable, and we may be hurt. If our cause or idea is rejected we may personally feel rejected. If we reveal ourselves we may be misunderstood or used. Giving ourselves in marriage or in commitment to any cause may be frightening; and some of us would rather give money and let the others get on the firing line. Some people would rather move slowly and cautiously; for them money may be the beginning stage of a form of self-commitment, but it may also be an end in itself and a barrier to self-involvement. As we mature as a people and as Christians it becomes easier to give of ourselves to Christ's cause along with our money.

I know of a man who gives generously to the church from his abundance of wealth. He is ostentatious in his giving and lets it be known that he is a substantial contributor to the budget of the church. Why does he need to make such a display? The major reason for this self-aggrandizement is probably that he does not think he is worthy of being loved for who he is. He is insecure, and his money has made him feel significant and worthy of respect, if not affection. The man who bases his personal worth on material things frequently uses this material advantage to convince others of his value as a person.

We are all social creatures and are usually very sensitive to what others think about us. Just knowing that the church clerk, secretary, and pastor will see our financial statement from the church at the end of the year may be enough to increase our giving to our church. This yearly statement may be interpreted as a reflection of our financial status, our interest in the cause of the church, and even our spirituality. I have often wondered what the financial status of many churches would be if no one was ever to find out what each member gave!

The motives of the little girl who drops her neat white Sunday school envelope in the plate, or of the man who pulls out his billfold and takes out a dollar bill and drops it into the offering basket when it is passed, or of the man and wife who systematically look at the various needs of the church around the world and divide up their modest contribution accordingly, are difficult to analyze. We do know that there are few if any pure altruistic motives for giving; at best we give from a combination of motives, some Christian, some self-centered, and some unconscious.

25

We know that our childhood experiences mold both our concepts about God and our values about giving, and that they consciously and unconsciously motivate us all of our lives. Yet knowing all of this the true Christian has the pervading belief that his love for the Savior, although certainly mixed in with his other motives, is the major reason why he gives to Christian causes, and that Christ's cause will ultimately be served.

One day my daughter came home from school with an orange-colored, twisted hunk of clay which she had baked in a kiln. It vaguely resembled an ashtray and we still display it proudly. I received it with admiration and love because it was something my daughter had made for me. It was not worth anything financially but it was her work, the best she could do, and it was an extension of herself for me.

I suppose the Christian must see himself in the position of my daughter. After realizing that there are no pure motives, including his own, he must still go ahead and give himself and his material wealth. But perhaps money has been a real hindrance in our concept of giving. What God, like any father, may prefer more than anything from us may be a twisted, handmade ashtray or a stick-man picture, and a good-night hug.

BIBLIOGRAPHY

Mowrer, O. Hobart. "Payment or Repayment?" *American Psychologist, XVIII,* No. 9 (Sept. 1963).

Tournier, Paul. *The Meaning of Gifts.* Richmond, Va.: John Knox Press, 1963.

SPIRITUAL GUIDANCE

Some people, in the name of Christianity, use a form of theistic magic to help escape the responsibility of making a decision.

3

SPIRITUAL GUIDANCE

Emotion or Decision?

ONE of my tasks as a clinical psychologist is to help people understand themselves in the person-to-person encounter called psychotherapy. During the course of treatment the patient is assisted in clarifying his conscious motives. He is encouraged to bring his hidden, unconscious motives and impulses to consciousness. He is also helped to relate his past experiences to his present behavior. This process tends to bring order out of chaos, understanding out of hopeless confusion, peace of mind out of fear, and strength out of weakness.

When we begin to understand the myriad relationships that exist between past experience and present behavior, we are confronted with the obvious fact that man functions quite lawfully. Since man's behavior appears lawful, it can be understood and predicted, once the laws are uncovered. The task of contemporary psychology is to uncover these laws and to help apply them in the mental health clinic, in industry, international relations, etc. I will consider this topic further in a later chapter.

As Christians, we must ask if this procedure also holds true for Christian religious experience. In the light of past experience, present physiological and emotional states, is personal religious experience understandable? I personally believe that an understanding of our past experiences can assist us in interpreting behavior, including our highest religious impulses.

Many Christians resist any such interpretation because they believe that their personal experiences are of such a spiritual nature that they are beyond the probing analysis of the psychologist. Perhaps this is partially true, but I believe the psychologist can give us insight into our understanding of some "spiritual" behavior which is often perplexing and misinterpreted. Hopefully this chapter may expand the understanding of one of these religious experiences, a phenomenon which is typically called "God's leading."

It is obvious to most people that our aspirations, self-concepts, parental expectations, fears, prejudices, disappointments, and present physical conditions are interwoven into the fabric of every decision of life. These decisions also include those which are classified under the heading of "God's guidance."

Let me illustrate this point with a hypothetical case. John Andrews is a teenager participating in a Sunday evening youth meeting at church. During the service, gospel choruses are sung, a prayer is offered, and a forty-five-minute talk is given by a visiting speaker on the topic of "Commitment to Christ." After presenting the hazards inherent in lack of commitment to God, the speaker reads a few verses from the Bible and tells what positive, pleasurable things happen to those who commit themselves to Christ. After the final appeal to these high school students to give everything to God, the speaker offers them an opportunity to respond quietly to the plea. Then he requests that those who have made such a decision for Christ declare it openly by going to the front of the room. John, aware of much inner tension, which he interprets as the internal leading of the Holy Spirit, makes an open declaration of his commitment to God; he even feels compelled to say that he believes God is calling him to the ministry.

Is this simple act of commitment and vocational choice God's leading, or is it a psychological phenomenon, or both? Perhaps it is a pure act of faith and trust in light of God's illumination; but it may be much more complex than this, and probably always is.

Apart from the usual "spiritual" interpretation, what might have been some of the developmental and motivational factors in John's decision? There were the pressures of the meeting itself with the influences of the pulsating gospel choruses, and the message which probably appealed heavily to John's fears, hopes, and personal incongruities.

What other factors might there have been?

Perhaps John had been competing with another brother for the affection of his parents. It is possible that, consciously or unconsciously, he knew his parents wanted more than anything else a boy dedicated to God; and the ultimate form of dedication would be a "call to full-time Christian service." A decision could be used to gain the limelight from his brother. Or this decision may have been the culmination of implicit and explicit coercion from the parents during most of John's life. The parents' prayers, conversations, and hopes may have come to a culmination at this point in his life.

Another factor could have been that the pastor of the congregation had been placed on a pedestal before John all his life, and he unconsciously wished to have the same place of importance in the thoughts of others. Such a position would be a form of compensation, to overcome a sense of inferiority and inadequacy.

The tension experienced, and interpreted as the leading of the Holy Spirit, may have been John's awareness of the great discrepancy between his values and his actual behavior which tended to produce guilt feelings, the results of which were anxiety and depression. John might think that this "ultimate" act of commitment, with its implicit confession and catharsis, would reduce the anxiety and depression. And this probably would happen because confession and commitment are good therapeutic agents. John probably also hoped that the commitment would give him the strength to bring harmony between his behavior and his ideals, which it probably would not do for any sustained period of time.

It is not unlikely that this adolescent was struggling with the normal developing sexual impulses which seem at times overwhelming and tend to cause many guilt feelings. Some adolescents choose the ministry or a vocation in missions because this is the most extreme form of self-commitment they can make. They hope that in so doing God will help them overcome their "sinful" sexual preoccupations. Other factors which might have been influential in this choice were pressure from peers, perhaps a girl friend who wanted to transform him, the desire to feel superior, or exhibitionistic tendencies.

It is obvious that any choice, be it in a secular or a religious context, is influenced by a multiple number of motives, developmental experiences, attitudes, and fears. The only way to minimize the extreme influences of the unconscious factors is to become aware of ourselves and of the subtle psychological defenses which we have used to protect ourselves from being hurt. The more conscious we are of the forces which clamor to be heard in the process of decision making, the more maturely we can respond to the situation.

There are always a few persons who tend to run away from decision making. These are the individuals who have had decisions made for them all of their lives by parents who encouraged infantile dependence; or they may be so insecure and unsure of themselves that to make a decision demands more self-confidence than they have. The methods used to avoid decision making are many.

Some people, in the name of Christianity, use a form of *theistic magic* to help escape the responsibility of making a decision. Occasionally we hear of the individual who randomly opens the Scriptures and uses the first verse that comes to his attention as the answer to his problem. Others may look for cues in nature or in their interpersonal relationships as guideposts, e.g., "The next person that comes into the room will hold the key to my problem." I once read of a man who said he would make a certain decision if the telephone rang within a given period of time. These are some of the devices used to avoid confronting an issue and making a decision in the light of mature reflection.

I do not mean to imply, however, that God has not revealed himself and his program in unconventional ways, but such instances are rare. To bypass the processes of reason and mature reflection opens the door to decisions which are dominated by unconscious motives, pressures of the moment, and changeable emotions. Such decisions may even be opposed to Biblical directives and contrary to the well-being of humanity.

Many professional psychiatrists and psychologists have pointed out that man's concept of God and his concept of his own father are often closely interrelated. As a matter of fact, we are admonished by the Bible to use the father as a teaching example of the Eternal God, i.e., "Our Father who art in heaven." Those who find decision making difficult may be tempted to confuse God and father; they regress to an immature behavior pattern by asking God, made in the image of their father, to make the decision for them. Many believe that the answers are communicated from this "heavenly father" via our emotions; they make such a statement as "I feel that God led me to do this."

Those who look to their emotions as indicators of God's response expose themselves to many confusing and distressing problems. From a theological point of view there is often the temptation to equate one's feelings with the working of God's Spirit, a presupposition that is unwarranted and Scripturally unfounded.

After an evening service one Sunday, the pastor told me that he had really felt the Holy Spirit's presence that night. As I analyzed the situation, my interpretation was different. The pastor's message touched on basic human needs, he related Scripture to these needs, he was well prepared and fluent in his delivery, and had rapport with his audience. Indeed, God's Spirit may have influenced members of his congregation when they were confronted with the Word of God in the light of their needs To equate emotional rapport, however, with the working of God's Spirit is hazardous, and the pastor expressed a naïvete in his understanding of the greatness and mystery of the working of the Third Person of the Trinity.

From a psychological point of view the emotions often can mislead because they are volatile, dependent upon physical and environmental conditions, and susceptible to conscious and unconscious manipulations by ourselves and by others. It is easy to allow the emotions to overwhelm the rational processes, permitting a person to become the victim of his fickle whims. I am not disparaging feeling in the healthy, mature Christian experience, but I believe that such feeling should be tested by Biblical truth, be consistent with a Biblical perspective, and be kept in balance with mature reason.

Some Christians live totally in their emotions. They talk incessantly about their feelings: "I feel God's presence moment by moment"; "I feel God led me to this place"; "I felt God led me to say that." The Christian life obviously cannot and should not be separated from the emotions. The gospel with its story of love, selfless giving, and resurrection demands an emotional response from the believer. But a healthy balance of "believing" and "feeling" is essential. I personally enjoy hearing a person state that he is motivated because he *believes* it is right rather than that he "feels" it is right.

Since emotions can be very misleading, it is probably true that rational judgments made after much contemplation will represent our true character and attitude. They will be less likely to lead to behavior which we will later regret, or which may be contradictory to Biblical direction.

It has been said that to live is to choose. One of the realities of life is that we constantly make decisions, big and small. The healthy, mature person does not avoid decision making. He becomes aware of the available facts, discovers the alternatives, makes a decision, reevaluates the decision in light of further information, and may change the decision if it is necessary and possible.

The person who commits himself to the missionary enterprise may find, after some experience on the field, that he does not fit into that context. The adjustments to a new culture may be too difficult, or the ability to endure the demands of a full-time evangelistic effort may be more than he can handle. Such a person should have the psychological freedom to reevaluate his decision, change his mind, and return home to a different occupation. We apparently can accept this principle in every phase of life except "full-time" Christian involvements. Some Christian communities implicitly or explicitly challenge one's "spirituality" if a decision is made to leave the vocation of missions or of the ministry. For fear of this rejection—and fear that indeed these accusations may be true—many persist in their efforts in spite of obvious indications that they should be considering a new course of action.

What makes decision making different for the Christian is the fact that the Biblical perspective becomes an integral part of the process. As God illuminates Holy Scripture, we can apply it to life, to the multiple number of choices which confront us. What I would encourage is mature, rational decision making by Christians who have committed themselves to Christ and who are willing to keep the Scriptures before them as a significant element in the decision-making process.

One important fact which we have already noted about ourselves is that we do very little, if anything, from pure motives. I am often motivated to do something not only because it is right, Christian, and healthy, but also because it will help me or elevate me in a self-centered way. As Christians we must all realize that our motives seldom are pure, and we must accept this fact as part of our humanity. Then even though the dilemma has not been resolved, it will be clear and open to us, and we can act.

In many instances, however, we are not aware of our motives because they are unconscious and beyond our ability to grasp. I am sure that some *strong* defenders of the faith are expressing their unconscious hostility through their caustic verbal assaults on those who do not share their beliefs. They act in the name of Christianity, but out of unconscious angry feelings. I often find it true of myself; when I am angry I tend to defend Christian orthodoxy much more strongly and have less respect for the opinions and feelings of others. To confess that my defense of Christianity has been in large measure the result of my frustration with my children (or with someone else) is a hard but necessary admission I must sometimes make.

It has been obvious to Christians throughout the history

35

of the Church that ascertaining God's guidance in the affairs of life is difficult, and that many errors are made. Many Christians have rested in the providential care of God. They realize that he is sovereign, he honors the intent of the believer, and prospers the ministry of his Word and the display of Christian love wherever it is exhibited. What God wants and has promised to bless is the man truly committed to him and anxious to do what is true in the light of Biblical revelation and mature reflection.

GUILT

It is obvious that there is a fine balance between too severe a conscience and too little. It is at this point that the Christian parent must identify with the contemporary psychologist in order to understand what is meant by the Biblical injunction to "bring up a child in the way he should go."

4.

GUILT

Conscience or Hangups?

"I've confessed my sin to God many times, but I still feel so guilty and dirty." These were the words of a young college girl who had been subjected to the sexual exploits of a neurotic father since she was thirteen years old. Although circumstances in general may not be as grotesque as this, she expressed a common problem of mankind: "I feel so guilty and dirty."

The professional psychotherapist, pastor, or any person who counsels, soon learns that often behind socially acceptable façades people are weighed down, and occasionally crushed, with the load of guilt feelings. This burden may represent almost any form of thought or behavior which violates some conscious or unconscious value system. I am reminded of another college girl who wondered if God would forgive her for some "grave misdeeds," i.e., attending the senior prom and holding hands with her escort. Others may feel guilty for overeating, procrastination, angry feelings, or inconsistency.

We need to keep in mind that a person may feel guilty for almost anything, and that this feeling may or may not be related to a Biblical view of guilt. A person may suffer from guilt feelings for attending a movie or playing cards, but he may have no negative emotional reaction to destroying another's reputation through vengeful gossip. The Christian must always struggle to be sure he is expressing a Biblical ethic rather than merely the pattern of the culture in which he lives.

In the course of my experiences as a clinical psychologist, I have had the opportunity of seeing many patients in mental hospitals. As I have walked through the wards in these hospitals, seeing the deep suffering and the patients' withdrawal from reality into their own private worlds, I have asked over and over again, *Why?* What happened to produce such sickness? What can be done to bring healing to this mass of sick humanity? In the many volumes which present research and theory concerning these various maladies, there is a recurring theme: guilt feelings can harm and possibly destroy the dynamic personality structure. A man can bend and break under the consequences of a violated conscience.

The fact that guilt feelings tend to produce disorders in the human psyche appears universally accepted in the mental health professions. Leslie Weatherhead, a pioneer in the field of pastoral psychology, has said: "In all psychotherapeutic practice it is found that the sense of guilt plays a large part. Sometimes, indeed, guilt, either conscious or repressed, is a determining factor in neurosis, and in the writer's own experiences a sense of guilt has frequently been responsible for the onset of serious physical symptoms."[1]

O. H. Mowrer, a psychologist of repute, states: "Where neurosis or psychosis is purely functional (as it usually is), the individual, I believe, always has a hidden history of serious misconduct which has not been adequately compensated and 'redeemed.' "[2]

Ernest White, a British psychiatrist, in his book *Chris-*

[1] *Psychology, Religion, and Healing*, p. 316.
[2] *The Crisis in Psychiatry and Religion*, p. 57.

tian Life and the Unconscious, says: "I have often discovered, especially in analysis of patients with high moral standards, that emotional and physical symptoms have their origin, at least in part, in some unconfessed and unforgiven sin which they have tried to forget or brush aside as being of no consequence" (p. 156).

We must be cautious at this point lest we take an easy road, as Mowrer tends to do, and say that this is the only reason for all mental disturbance. This, in my opinion, would be a grave error and a distortion of our present knowledge of mental illness, because it does not account for the neuroses which are the result of inadequate parent-child relationships. As one trained in child psychology it would usually be professionally inappropriate for me to point to a child's misbehavior as *the cause* of his problems. For example, a child who is tense, fidgety, and at times incorrigible is more likely to be afraid of his rage impulses and lack of control than to be experiencing guilt feelings.

What does a person mean when he says he feels guilty? Usually he means that he feels depressed and has a vague sense of unworthiness because of a violated conscience. How is this conscience developed, and why the depression?

The conscience is the by-product of two sources. First, a child identifies with some significant person in his development, usually a parent of the same sex, so that the child becomes like this person in behavior and thought to the extent of holding similar values. Second, a person incorporates a value system which is stamped in via punishment for violation of parental expectations.

In the first method the model with whom the child identifies, frequently called the "ego ideal," rewards the child for behavior which is similar to his own. As a result of this reward, the child reproduces the same behavior until it becomes a part of his self-concept. When a child shares a toy or some candy with another child, he is frequently rewarded with some form of pleasant reinforcement such as a compliment, a pat on the head, or even another piece of candy. If this type of behavior is consistently reinforced, the child will do it over and over again until it becomes part of his value system. The result of a violation to this part of the individual's value system is a mild feeling of regret for having done something which makes him less than his model, but no severe form of self-incrimination and depression appears.

The child begins to identify with one of the parents at an early age, and the evidences of this identification are many. The boy plays with baseballs and the girl with dolls; the boy plays fireman and the girl becomes an imaginary ballet star; the boy likes to wrestle and the girl to read. This process of identification also carries over to value systems. The boy not only walks and talks like his dad, he also thinks like him, and his attitudes and values will become like his dad's. To be like Dad and to be praised for this resemblance is nearly the highest reward a child can receive.

Ernest White has made the suggestion that this is how the conscience of a mature Christian should develop. Christ becomes the ego ideal, and the Christian wants to be like him. Through the confrontation of the Word of God, prayer, and worship, the Christian more and more assumes the "mind of Christ." This tends to produce a mature conscience and a mentally healthy one. Of the two forms of conscience development, the identification with the ego ideal is by far the more desirable because it has little of the self-punitive emotions connected with it.

The second form of conscience development is the result of punishment. It is typical in many families to punish a child, either physically or by the withdrawal of love and approval, when he does something of which the parents disapprove. The child soon learns that certain behavior is associated with punishment or other forms of rejection. What happens after this pattern is well ingrained and the value system which we call a conscience is violated and the parents do not punish? The person will punish himself.

Depression is one basic form of self-punishment and usually is accompanied by self-castigation and self-rejection. When we feel guilty we tend to become moody and to distort reality through the gray glasses of pessimism. The world appears to fall apart, and death and despair are the prime factors in life. Interpersonal relationships are reduced to manipulations, and we reduce our personal worth to nothing. While in this state we wonder how anyone could love us because we are so unlovable, and we proceed to live in a world of self-depreciation and personal rejection.

Self-punishment may even result in self-inflicted physical harm in an accident. It has been suggested that persons who are accident prone feel chronically guilty and are constantly punishing themselves. One day one of my students had accidentally walked into a car, injuring her leg rather seriously. I made the comment in jest, but it was full of psychological meaning, that she now had some credit for a few sins in the future. The pain she was then suffering would not only reduce her present guilt feelings (assuming she felt guilty) but could possibly reduce the impact of future guilt feelings.

If we can understand the self-punitive results of violating a part of the individual's value system, we can begin to see the basic problem behind some forms of severe depression. Some people suffer under the burden of deep guilt feelings but are not aware of the source of these feelings. The offenses are "unconscious," but the guilt feelings are still there

Every human being has an array of memories he has repressed into the unconscious, many of which tend to be guilt producing. The adult who as a child had fantasies of killing a competitive brother or sister may suffer depression later when events of life stimulate these unconscious memories. Perhaps the death of this competitive brother or sister may trigger an extraordinary amount of depression. In essence the individual is punishing himself for the unconscious wishes of his youth. The obvious source of his depression would be the loss of his brother through death, but the core of the severe depression is much deeper and more serious.

An adequate conscience is obviously necessary for the continuation of society and for helping the child to deal with his own socially unacceptable impulses. The important question is, how much of a conscience is mentally healthy? Where there is little conscience, we have the sociopath who has little inner control and is in continual conflict with society. On the other side of the fence we see those who suffer from the oppression of too strict a conscience. These people tend to be depressed and unproductive; they live in continual fear of their thoughts and behavior lest the conscience

43

be violated and self-condemnation and depression gush forth. They so dissipate their energies in morbid introspection and avoiding "wrong" behavior by suppressing or denying basic human impulses, that they have no energy left for constructive creative effort.

I am reminded of a girl in psychotherapy who seemed to enjoy telling how bad and inadequate she was and how she felt no one could love her. She would tell many stories which were basically self-punitive. In her work she would make obvious mistakes so that her employer would become angry with her; thus she would receive the punishment which she felt was coming to her. Once she filed her toenails to the quick until they bled—another incident of self-punishment.

When she began to think that she was possibly worthy of love, she felt very guilty for these thoughts. Before going to bed at night she would pinch herself so severely that she cried in order to assuage her guilt feelings brought on by the belief that she might be lovable. Frequently she would say things to anger her friends, to prove to herself that she really was not worthy of friendship.

What produces such a severe conscience? Perhaps a glimpse of her home may be of help. She related to me the joy she had when she was made valedictorian of her high school class. She anxiously awaited her parents' approval, especially her father's, for whom she had spent extra hours of study. She wanted his approval more than anything else in the world and hoped for his praise—but he never said anything to her about the honor. When asked about it later, he said that he did not want his daughter to become proud because this would be unchristian. He felt that if he praised her she would not accept her ability as a "gift from God" but might take the glory for herself.

An extreme case, yes, but often in the extreme cases we can see the minor distortions in the developmental processes which plague us all. It is obvious that there is a fine balance between too severe a conscience and too little. It is at this point that the Christian parent must identify with the contemporary psychologist in order to understand what is meant by the Biblical injunction to "bring up a child in the way he should go." We see again and again many

Christians with great creative potential crushed under the oppression of too severe a conscience; we are confronted with one of the tragedies of segments of modern Christianity—people weighed down with an immature, overbearing conscience.

We must seek to develop mature consciences—through mature reflection and a healthy Christian world-life perspective—consciences which give us guidelines for living but set us free to explore and to appreciate ourselves and the world in which we live. Paul Tournier, in his excellent volume *Guilt and Grace*, differentiates between mature and immature guilt like this: "For true guilt is precisely the failure to dare to be oneself. It is the fear of other people's judgment that prevents us from being ourselves, from showing ourselves as we really are, from showing our tastes, our desires, our convictions, from developing ourselves and from expanding freely according to our own natures" (p. 17).

The Christian church throughout the centuries has been known for its message of forgiveness through God's grace. The church must continue to present this good news with clarity because it touches one of man's basic needs—the need to be freed from guilt feelings. As we read Psalm 51, David's great psalm of confession, we sense the therapeutic side effects. As David asks for God's forgiveness, we can almost feel the sense of inner peace which he probably experienced.

The church today also has the responsibility of communicating a truly Christian ethic, separated from cultural distortions, so that men will not suffer needlessly. The Christian church can help to free men from the needless burden of guilt feelings and point them to a mature Christian ethic with its positive counterparts in the emotional life of man.

BIBLIOGRAPHY

Mowrer, O. Hobart. *The Crisis in Psychiatry and Religion*. New York: D. Van Nostrand Co., Inc., 1961.
Tournier, Paul. *Guilt and Grace*. New York: Harper & Row, Inc., 1962.

Weatherhead, Leslie D. *Psychology, Religion, and Healing.*
New York: Abingdon Press, 1951.
White, Ernest. *Christian Life and the Unconscious.* New York:
Harper & Row, Inc., 1955.

WORSHIP

If a smorgasbord of worship services were laid out before a potential worshiper, which ones would he choose and why? Would he choose liturgy over gusto? Would he choose J. S. Bach or Fanny Crosby in musical selection? Would he choose hand-raising and foot-tapping to kneeling and prayer-book reciting?

. . . . . .

The great miracle is that the same God is worshiped in all these ways.

5

WORSHIP

J. S. Bach or Fanny Crosby?

A FRIEND of mine related an experience he had had during a worship service which exemplifies some of the problems related to the psychology of worship. He had just participated in a service quite different from the church experiences in his past; he found the service so strange that he felt most uncomfortable. He had been brought up to appreciate a very casual form of worship service, one that stressed spontaneity, hearty singing, and personalized messages from the pulpit calling for clear-cut and strong personal response. His home church building had few, if any, religious symbols in it, and was noted for its functional qualities rather than its aesthetic characteristics.

The church he had visited followed a carefully planned liturgy which had a long historical heritage and placed much emphasis on corporate confession and praise to God. On this particular occasion the sacrament of communion was served in a very different manner from any he had previously experienced. The church building was of modern architectural design; at the front it had an altar with many Christian symbols to add to the worship experience. Although it was a Protestant service and the worshipers were of approximately the same social status as my friend, his reaction to the service was that it was "cold" and seemed to lack "relevance" and personal meaning for him.

Here is an example of a Christian who purposefully sets out to worship but finds the setting and format of the service a detriment rather than a stimulant to his ability to worship. Why is this so? To say that the service was foreign to his experience is an obvious answer, but I wonder if it is enough to explain his negative reactions. Strangeness and lack of appreciation of the historical heritage of the service would cause some discomfort and perhaps dislike, but there are some deeper underlying problems.

If a smorgasbord of worship services were laid out before a potential worshiper, which ones would he choose and why? Would he choose liturgy over gusto? Would he choose J. S. Bach or Fanny Crosby in musical selection? Would he choose hand-raising and foot-tapping to kneeling and prayer-book reciting? This imaginary smorgasbord illustrates some of the problems which face the Christian community in the choice of forms of worship—problems which I would like to point out.

What are some of the factors involved in the choice of one form of worship over another—apart from the all-important factors of familiar tradition and custom? Most persons attend the church of their parents; this fact cannot be minimized. A child who grows up in a Lutheran church will tend to stay in the Lutheran church and probably worships meaningfully in it. The same is true for Baptists, Episcopalians, Presbyterians, Pentecostals, etc. There is great security and comfort in the familiar, especially if it unites the person's childhood and nostalgic past with the present worship format. To sing the songs of youth and to sit in a church like the one back home can often revitalize many positive emotions.

While this link with the past may prove psychologically satisfying to some, it may not satisfy those who are inquisitive, thoughtful, or those who reject the truisms and traditions of their parents. We who work with college students find that there are always some who inquisitively test a variety of worship experiences. Of these, many choose a form of worship experience, and possibly a theological position, quite different from the traditions of their family. Those who appear most likely to change have been brought up under the more casual form of worship service such as is found in many Baptist, independent, or Pentecostal churches. The tendency is to move toward more liturgy, symbolism, and corporate confession and praise.

Recently I heard of an incident in a college with a long fundamentalist heritage which illustrates the intensity of feelings connected with worship traditions. Some of the students wanted to place a large cross as a backdrop for the daily chapel service. There were strong sentiments for and against the inclusion of this Christian symbol in the service. Reasons were given for the exclusion of the cross, but underneath one could sense emotions which reflected strong Protestant and anti-Catholic sentiments as well as a fear that the preaching element of the service would be minimized. In other words, some people fear that the human being cannot worship meaningfully without a strong directive from the pulpit. Some people apparently do not feel they have worshiped unless a preacher taps some emotion such as fear, guilt, or anger. To respond only to the Word sung or the Word read seems inadequate.

J. B. Pratt makes a distinction between objective and subjective religion—a point which must be considered in any discussion of worship. Objective worship is centered in the adoration and praise of God; subjective worship is centered in the stimulation and edification of the worshiper. Although an adequate worship service will contain both elements, it is obvious that some services tend to stress one over the other.

It is my observation that the less emphasis there is on liturgy and the more casual the service, the greater is the stress on subjective worship. In subjective worship the worshiper does not believe he has worshiped unless he has undergone some "feeling" experience. Unless some memories of his past are tapped, unless some chords of disharmony are plucked, unless some challenge for personal piety is given, the person feels let down; he may even wonder "if God's Spirit was there." If this is one's orientation, he will

51

more than likely attend services where preaching and music magnify subjective feelings.

In his book *How to Become a Bishop Without Being Religious,* Charles Smith focuses attention on the selection of hymns which are meant to magnify the subjective element of worship, which stress personal feelings and trigger memories of childhood. Accompanying this choice is the minimizing of hymns which are basically outgoing and God-directed. If a person does not believe he has worshiped unless a high level of feeling accompanies the act of worship, he will tend to gravitate toward the less liturgical worship service.

People will tend to choose the type of worship service which seems to parallel their needs. I am reminded of the young man who was brought up in a rigidly structured Christian home. During his struggles for a personal identity during college, he almost discarded Christianity. The reasons he gave for his rejection were rather typical: the irrelevance of Christianity to the needs of mankind, the gross inconsistencies of Christians, the inability of Christianity to meet the needs of social problems of humanity which he concluded were racial strife, war, pain, and poverty. Basically he had decided to live a secular existence. Underneath the reasons the young man gave, however, he was saying that the God with whom he was familiar had nothing to say to him and his personal needs.

This young man was brought up in a home where he was given conditional love, especially by his father. If he did what was expected, he would be given affection; if he was not the perfect child, love would be withdrawn. As a youth, he lived in continual fear lest he offend this aggressive, withdrawn and punitive father. The church he attended pictured God in somewhat the same way: a God who is basically hostile and punitive, but who would love him if he were obedient to Him. The parallels between the father who gave conditional love and the God who gave conditional love were obvious and overruled any suggestion that God was not like the father, a natural psychological parallel.

In his struggles for autonomy from his parents, especially his father, this young man withdrew from the church. In the course of his separation struggles he became involved in psychotherapy where he was given unconditional love by a male therapist. Against this background of unconditional love, he was able to reconsider Christianity. In the process he chose to attend a church, very different from his childhood church, which tended to emphasize that God loves unconditionally, that God recognizes human frailty and sinfulness but still loves through it all. In essence the young man chose a church and a form of worship which consistently pointed to his worth and value rather than his failures and sinfulness. The emphasis which paralleled his needs determined his choice of church and worship service.

It is the frustrated, hostile persons who complain that the preacher does not preach about hell enough. They miss the vicarious enjoyment of hearing how bad the parishioners are and that they will go to hell if they do not respond. The need to express hostility is reflected in the type of sermon topics.

Whether one prefers the King James Version or the Phillips translation, whether one prefers spontaneous or read prayers, whether one responds to a cross in the church sanctuary with pleasure or pain, whether one prefers "Heavenly Sunshine" or the "Gloria Patri" depends upon many variables which must be considered in evaluating one's choice of worship. Differences of personality, past experience, ability to respond aesthetically, cultural level—all are part of the choice of worship. To pass a value judgment in preferring one over the other would be most difficult; people choose churches, theological emphases, and modes of worship on many different criteria, and to each their criteria appear to be the best. The great miracle is that the same God is worshiped in all these ways.

BIBLIOGRAPHY

Pratt, James B. *The Religious Consciousness: A Psychological Study*. New York: The Macmillan Company, 1920.
Smith, Charles M. *How to Become a Bishop Without Being Religious*. New York: Doubleday & Co., 1965.

PRAYER

We are usually painfully aware of our human limitations and weaknesses, but rarely do we become aware of our extraordinary potentials.

6.

PRAYER

To What Kind of God?

THE Christian should be actively engaged in prayer. This is commanded explicitly and implicitly in the Scriptures. Christ is our model and we have several recorded accounts of his prayer life. Throughout history Christians have found in prayer strength, courage, hope, succor, peace, and faith. In prayerful introspection we are confronted with ourselves, our self-centeredness, our potential, our capacities for love and for destructiveness, our estrangement from ourselves and from our fellow men. In prayer we confess our failures, plead for strength to help overcome our myriad weaknesses, lift petitions for help and salvation for loved ones, and ask for the growth of God's Kingdom. Prayer is often a period of ruthless self-probing when a man is as honest with himself as is possible. Our games of self-deception tend to be minimized as we confront our humanness and our need for God's grace.

The Christian also knows the barrenness of much praying, the perfunctory words and repetition which, like any habit, are frequently void of meaning. Yet the claim of all Christendom is that man and God meet in prayer, and that this experience is very personal and often beyond descriptive analysis. David described one of his experiences like this: "I waited patiently for the Lord; and he inclined unto me, and heard my cry. He brought me up also out of an horrible pit, out of the miry clay, and set my feet upon a rock, and established my goings" (Psalm 40:1–2).

In his attempt to investigate all of man's behavior, the psychologist has included prayer in his research, even though it is intensely personal and people often find it difficult to discuss their experiences. Because of its universal character, prayer is important and must be investigated. The purpose of this chapter is to bring to the attention of the Christian some of the findings about the phenomenon of prayer which the psychologists have uncovered. Such a discussion, hopefully, should enable the Christian to pray more intelligently.

Man is very complex. There are areas of his behavior which have barely been penetrated by the investigative skills of the psychologist. Such areas as hypnotism, extrasensory perception, conversion, and prayer point to the great potential in man, but they are little understood. We are usually painfully aware of our human limitations and weaknesses, but rarely do we become aware of our extraordinary potentials. That man does have vast potential should make the Christian appreciate both himself and his Creator more.

Perhaps I can illustrate man's potential by referring to the phenomenon of hypnotism. Under hypnotic suggestion people can see and feel things which are not there, or be oblivious of things that are there.

In classroom demonstrations I have hypnotized students and told them that when they awoke they would not see me until they were given a particular cue. When they awoke, they would look around and often ask the other students where I was, even though I was standing immediately in front of them. The state would continue until the hypnotic suggestion was broken by the appropriate cue. What these students did, purely by the power of suggestion, was to block a portion of the external world out of their consciousness.

Under the influence of hypnotic suggestion people can do some extraordinary things. They can undergo painless childbirth and surgery, can break chronic habit patterns, and incorporate new behavior and thought patterns into their repertoire of responses. Persons under hypnotic influence can read pages of detailed information and reproduce it verbatim at a later time.

From these examples we can begin to sense something of man's great potential—man who is made in the image of God. If the potential can be appreciated by the Christian, the psychological perspective on prayer can be more meaningful.

Since prayer is not uniquely a Christian phenomenon, the psychologist must investigate prayer behavior wherever it is found. It could be defined as communion with a God, a God who "is there." Whether this is a spontaneous cry for help or a formal utterance, it is directed to the God who is believed to be hearing and present. One must therefore consider the characteristics of the God who is there.

Each Christian conceives of God in a different way, and prays accordingly. His concept comes from a variety of concrete experiences of life. Since each individual has unique experiences, his concept of God will never be identical with that of another person. God may be conceived of as a tyrant, a beneficent companion, a detached creator, a senile man, or a vigorous, concerned friend. What kind of God you believe is there influences how, and if, you pray.

Christ taught his disciples to pray, "Our Father who art in heaven." He used one of the best ways of teaching children about God—that is making parallels between the child's father and God. Unfortunately, many persons have childhood experiences with fathers which make it difficult, if not impossible, to pray adequately to God as heavenly Father. For some children the father may be nonexistent either through death, divorce, or separation. A few mothers live in a state of semi-prostitution and the children have seen a multitude of men in the house—it is almost impossible to imagine what these children think and feel when they hear someone pray "Our Father . . . ." The father figure may be an alcoholic, a self-preoccupied neurotic, or an authoritarian despot. He may be moody, aggressive, preferential in the treatment of his children, unforgiving.

The child who perceives God as a father who is detached will be reluctant to pray because he will expect God neither to hear nor care. If a child fears his father, he may withdraw from a God conceived in the father's image. Others may harbor conscious and unconscious hostility towards their father and may, therefore, be reticent to pray to any God who is like the father. The child who thinks of God as an unforgiving father will probably doubt that he will forgive an honest confession. The child whose father gave preferential treatment to other brothers or sisters may reject any approach to God out of chronic hostility toward the father.

These associations do not die with the end of childhood. One of the adult's big problems is that they carry over into his "adult" concepts of God. It is conceivable that some people should be encouraged to pray only to Christ and to make parallels between Christ and God, rather than between a father and God.

In this regard, the Catholics have a great psychological advantage. They pray to Mary, a mother symbol. A mother is usually more approachable, more empathetic than a father, less punitive, and often acts as an arbiter between the child and the father. Psychologically, therefore, it would be much easier to approach God the Father through the understanding mother figure.

One of the tasks of the Christian church is to present a Biblical view of God which will minimize the influence of a person's past harmful experiences. It is impossible to eliminate these perceptions completely, though, because we always see the present through the experiences of the past; but a thorough understanding of the Biblical doctrine of God can be of help. The person needs to know what kind of God is "there" when he enters into a prayer experience.

We can usually say that, when considered from a Biblical perspective, "our God is too small," and often distorted. As mature Christians we need to see God as the God of the

Old and New Testaments—the great Yahweh of the Old and the Christ of the New. Until we come to this maturity, our conceptualized God will be greatly distorted by our past experiences. The distortion will be reflected in our prayer life, and in our interpretations of the by-products of prayer. For instance, if we are afraid of God, we will probably come before Him in chronic meek confession; if we perceive God to be basically a loving God, we will tend to express appreciation for his love and care.

The definition of prayer stresses that prayer is a communion between God and man, a fellowship, an interaction with Deity. By its definition and by its nature prayer is subjective and very personal. In spite of this, a few comments should be made.

The interaction of prayer is often stated something like this: "God spoke to me this morning, and I to Him." What most people mean by such a statement is not that they sensorially heard a voice but that during the prayer experience a new self-awareness took place. Often during such a time of meditative introspection what someone has said or what has been learned or read in the Bible becomes personally relevant. To say that God "speaks to me" through the Word of God in its various forms (the Word spoken, the Word sung, the Word read) is understandable and consistent with historical, orthodox Christianity. On the other hand, it is probably a more accurate description to say that "the Scriptures were very meaningful to me during prayer"—a statement which will probably cause less confusion to the uninitiated. God in his providential care has chosen to use his Word to reveal himself, man's nature, and his purpose for man; this fact is crucial to our understanding of God's guidance and of our self-revelatory experiences during prayer.

It is often true that some people equate any insight and emotional response in the prayer experience as God's interaction with them. This interpretation often leads to confusion because emotions are volatile and fluctuating. They are susceptible to conscious and unconscious manipulations by ourselves and others, as we have already seen. This is the reason why some people say that their "prayers seem to

61

bounce off the ceiling." What they are really saying is that they did not feel anything while praying; therefore God must not have heard their prayers.

At other times a person may describe his prayer life as rich and meaningful; what he means is that his emotions have been aroused so that he *feels* something. Scripture demands that a man should pray, but makes no statement about how he must feel in order to be heard. It is important for the Christian to function on the level of belief rather than emotion when it comes to prayer. God says that He hears, and this is true whether a person feels that He does or not.

For some, this emotional experience in prayer becomes an apologetic for Christianity and a key to personal evangelism. The apologetic is often stated something like this: "I know Christ lives because I spoke to him this morning and he to me." Could devout believers of other religions make the same kind of statement? Do they get a similar emotional and personal feedback in the prayer experience? A well-read person could challenge the "I talked with God" apologetic by pointing out that the more mystical branches of most religions can say the same or similar things with all honesty. The Muslim or Buddhist could say that he, too, feels that he has communed with his God, his deity as he sees it from his own theological point of view.

Some persons ask whether prayer is only autosuggestion. It would be most presumptive to imply that prayer is nothing but autosuggestion, but to say that it is not in part autosuggestion would be inappropriate. Psychologists have learned from work with hypnotism that suggestion can play a very creative and important part in man's effective working. As a person prays for love he tends to become more loving; as he prays for peace of mind he begins to think peaceful thoughts. The "power of positive thinking" has a basis in fact. As the author of the book of Proverbs puts it: "As he thinketh within himself, so is he" (Proverbs 23:7).

Through the self-suggestive elements of prayer, a person is helped to set up new thought patterns which can increase personal confidence, change habit patterns, and positively reorient the person toward his fellow man. God made man so that he functions best as a praying, meditating being; so the Christian is commanded to be actively involved in prayer. What spiritual or psychological laws produce change should only be of tangential importance.

When a psychologist investigates prayer in its various forms and within its many religious contexts, he searches for common elements. Some of the common elements are the following:

Confession. Confession, either to another person or to God, has some psychological by-products. A relief from tension frequently follows this cathartic experience, accompanied by a reduction of internal conflict, a relief from self-punitive depression, and often a period of purposeful living. These are the by-products of being honest with ourselves in the presence of others, and occur in other contexts than prayer. In two of his books, *The New Group Therapy* and *The Crisis in Psychiatry and Religion*, O. H. Mowrer says that man needs to confess his sins openly—become openly honest with others. When this is done, the positive psychological by-products will ensue. Confession and honesty are therapeutic in any context, whether in group therapy, Alcoholics Anonymous, or prayer.

Renewal of energy. Prayer brings the renewal of energy for one's tasks. People often report new vigor and enthusiasm for the task at hand, or a new strength to face the unchangeable realities of existence.

Social sensitivity. As the result of prayer one becomes less self-centered and more aware of the struggles and dilemmas of people throughout the world.

Awareness of personal needs. A greater awareness of personal needs ensues when a person becomes honest with himself in prayer. He perceives the need for confession, restitution, God's forgiving grace, and sensitivity to man's human dilemma.

A readjusted hierarchy of values. As a person prays, his values are readjusted. Self-centered concerns, which before prayer seemed very important, become unimportant, and other-centered concerns become focal.

Fellowship. Man has a need for fellowship with other men and with God. This need is often met in prayer.

The Biblical statement that man is made in God's image has many profound implications. For one thing, it should give us sober pause before we discredit man or minimize his potential. We should be able to say with the psalmist: "I will praise thee; for I am fearfully and wonderfully made" (Psalm 139:14).

The belief that God intervenes and is involved in the lives of people is a basic tenet of Christianity. It is supported experientially by men of faith who have trusted God to help in their crisis experiences as well as in the daily affairs of life. The recorded history of the church presents many personal accounts of men who through prayer have found the help and strength to live vigorously, courageously and uprightly. For anyone to state categorically that prayer is only a personal introspective experience would be most presumptive and beyond the present knowledge of our vast universe. One would then have to deny the testimony of many who have experienced in their lives God's answer to prayer. On the other hand, the common psychological elements must be taken into account in a broad discussion of prayer.

The difference between the Christian and the non-Christian is not the psychological by-products of prayer but the God to whom one prays. For the Christian this is the God of the Bible. As the Master Designer, he made man and knows how man can work most efficiently. As part of his master plan, he ordained that man should be a praying creature, and that the psychological by-products of prayer would be helpful for man's highest functioning.

HOW FREE IS MAN?

A few Christians appear to live harmoniously with the deterministic hypothesis; they usually are Calvinistic in theology. They believe strongly in God's sovereignty and providential care, and stress education as a method of bringing a person to salvation in Christ.

7

HOW FREE IS MAN?

Determinism and the Christian

ONE of the most pressing problems confronting the Christian today, on a theoretical or philosophical level, is the question of determinism in its various forms. Since determinism is an underlying assumption in the natural and behavioral sciences, it influences consciously or unconsciously our world-life view.

Determinism—either social, psychological, or physical—implies that for any event there are antecedent causes. One can explain the movement of billiard balls on a table in terms of the energy used to set off the chain of events. In the same way the psychologist tries to explain human behavior in terms of lawful relationships between the past and present. For instance, claustrophobia (a fear of small enclosed places) may be related to a painful experience in youth, e.g., being locked in a closet by accident.

Most psychologists and social scientists presuppose that past experiences influence and often dictate future behavior. The only reason that one cannot predict human behavior with 100 percent accuracy, the social scientist often states, is that not all the laws which govern human behavior have been discovered. Also, at this stage in our understanding of man, even if the laws were known, there is no person knowledgeable enough to assemble the information into a conceptual package which matches man's complexity. This does not imply that the social scientists cannot predict human behavior, according to them, but their prognostications are usually framed in terms of probability statements.

For a Christian clinical psychologist, determinism presents a difficult theoretical problem. It also influences in a practical way my professional contacts with those who are in need of help. For the college student, determinism appears to be an insurmountable world-life view which necessarily influences the very core assumptions we make about ourselves and the world around us.

In his excellent discussion of the problem, Paul Meehl states: "Scientific naturalism philosophically underpinned by logical empiricism, often in an unquestioned and even unstated form, is today the strongest intellectual enemy of the church and among educated people gives the most powerful no to the church's proclamation."[1] He goes on to say: "Determinism and its (seeming) implications constitute for the psychologist both a scientific stumbling block in respect to miracles, conversion, and the action of God in history, and a moral stumbling block in regard to responsibility, choice, 'freedom,' election, and related concepts."[2]

The clinical psychologist, psychiatrist, social worker, or educator often makes predictions about human behavior in light of current and past knowledge of an individual. This procedure is commonly accepted; but the assumption underlying such predictions—i.e., psychological determinism—is seldom challenged. The clinical psychologist predicts what will happen to a patient if he is put back into the environment which caused the abnormal reaction. The educator predicts academic success from academic records, teachers' evaluations, and test findings, etc.

[1] *What, Then, Is Man?* p. 173.
[2] P. 174.

The pointed question which the Christian must ask is: "Is this true of religious experience also?" Can religious experience be predicted by a knowledge of the past? If it is true, then one might assert that a person's experiences which have been labeled uniquely Christian might not be of supernatural origin but be merely a by-product of the environmental influences at a particular moment. Many college students discuss their Christian experiences in terms of "being psyched out." Regrettably, prayer, conversion, meditation, and worship become to many just other examples of the overwhelming influence of the moment—an emotional chain reaction produced by the psychic machine. Why inject a supernatural element into the process? While the lawful psychological influences in religious experiences cannot be casually dismissed, the spiritual dimension must not be eliminated in favor of a fatalistic determinism.

The deterministic assumption underlying all of science is so ingrained in our culture that it is difficult for us to think differently. For instance, when we consider the problems of the inner city, we think of the causes which precipitated them. We hear of poverty, the lack of male examples, inferior education, or inadequate work opportunities as causes of the riots and despair which have torn our country. This is determinism in a practical context. It is stated that if these people in the inner city are to become productive citizens with personal dignity, their environment must be changed. Proposals for better schools, opportunities for employment, and so on are suggested. The underlying assumption is: change the causes and the behavior will also change.

Determinism, however, is *only an assumption* and should be accepted as such. It is a highly productive assumption, as the history of the natural and behavioral sciences proves, but it must be remembered that it is a hypothesis which is open for criticism and change if necessary—as is any theory. One finds, however, that in intellectual circles this hypothesis often becomes a metaphysical truism, a truth around which many have built a world-life view which they then defend as tenaciously as a Christian defends the deity of Christ. The raising of theory to truth makes the task of critical evaluation much more difficult. At the same time we must appreciate the high regard in which many hold this hypothesis.

Sigmund Freud was one of the most ardent and complete determinists. Anything which suggested freedom was to him only an illusion. A slip of the tongue, the act of forgetting, accidents, dreams—all were meaningful in the light of past experience and could be understood when these past influences were brought into consciousness. Freud extended this deterministic principle to religious behavior in such books as *Totem and Taboo* and *The Future of an Illusion.*

In contrast, the existentialist position states as a hypothesis that freedom to choose *against* one's past is crucial in understanding the nature of man. Although it is an oversimplification of the existentialist position, one could say that in the existentialist view man makes choices, is free to make these choices against the past, and is in control of the choice-making process. Man is therefore responsible for his behavior. The existentialists claim that awareness of this choice-making process and its counterpart, man's sense of responsibility, are two of the basic ingredients in man's humanness. To relegate man to the model of a deterministic machine is to make him an object and to dehumanize him.

In a sense, then, the person holding the existential viewpoint takes the other horn of the philosophical dilemma, and pushes determinism aside as incorrect and perhaps irrelevant. The conflict which exists between these two positions has lasted for many centuries and will probably continue for many more. Most psychologists, either pragmatically or theoretically, hold the existentialist assumption to be incongruous with the facts which support the deterministic presupposition.

Psychologists assume that man functions lawfully; therefore their task is to discover these laws and apply them to practical situations. When these laws are discovered and methods have been developed to measure the variables, man's behavior can be predicted and therefore controlled. The industrial psychologist is an example of those presently involved in this predictive process. The task of minimizing the number of misfits for certain jobs has saved business concerns large sums of money. The educator, clinical psychologist, social worker, psychiatrist, and researchers in human and animal behavior support the hypothesis that man functions systematically and is therefore predictable. Even though complete success in prediction is not possible, the determinist claims that this is the fault of the measuring instruments, or due to lack of knowledge of the variables; it cannot be traced to man's ability to live above or outside the context of lawfulness. There are various forms of the deterministic hypothesis of which Christians should be aware. The following ones are not meant to be inclusive, but they may help to clarify what is frequently unclear or at least unstated.

The first and most obvious position is *complete determinism*. This basically states that man is a creature of law and always will function within this lawful framework. His environment and heredity determine his choices. This is true even though he has an awareness of "freedom" in the choice-making process. This is the scientific, mechanistic view of man, and is frequently rejected by Christians. They claim that it reduces man to a machine and encourages fatalism. It is my belief that most of our social scientists accept this view and espouse it in the classroom as "truth."

A deist could accept this position by stating that God made the world to function lawfully and now remains detached from His handiwork. A theist who believes that God is actively involved in the affairs of men frequently finds this form of the hypothesis offensive because it allows no freedom for God's interaction with man and no room for human responsibility. A few Christians appear to live harmoniously with this theory; they usually are Calvinistic in theology. They believe strongly in God's sovereignty and providential care, and stress education as a method of bringing a person to salvation in Christ. They tend to emphasize the determinism present in Scripture, as for instance such verses as "Train up a child in the way he should go; and when he is old he will not depart from it," or "Whatsoever a man soweth that shall he also reap." Perhaps it is for this reason that psychology, psychiatry, and mental health facilities have been stressed by the groups heavily influenced by Calvin's theology. Their theology is consistent with the belief that man's behavior can be understood.

The second form of the hypothesis, *pragmatic determinism*, is held by many. This hypothesis states that determinism is helpful in research and theory, but it may not be the whole picture. Because determinism has been functional in our investigation of man, we will continue to assume its truth, but man is too complex to say that all his behavior can be determined; perhaps indeterminacy will be proven to exist. This is a wise, scientific attitude, but frequently it is held because the individuals espousing it have not taken the time and energy to think through the whole problem of the nature of man.

The Christian can hold this hypothesis and conduct productive creative research. The difficulty comes in dealing with the individual in the classroom or in the counseling room. Should the person be treated as a responsible choice-making person or as a victim of deterministic forces? Traditional psychoanalysis and much of the therapeutic world assumes the deterministic stance. One can assume this form of the hypothesis for research purposes, but in the therapeutic encounter it becomes a significant and pressing issue which cannot be ignored.

A third form of the hypothesis is proposed by Paul Tournier in his book *The Person Reborn*. It is his contention that *determinism and freedom are not opposites* but are both true at the same time. It is like looking at the proverbial elephant from two different vantage points. Man is obviously determined by his past, but at the same time he has the awareness of freedom to choose. Tournier claims that these are just two different ways of looking at the same behavior. This theory is appealing because one can seemingly hold to both positions without the conflict of choosing between them. Perhaps at this stage of our knowledge it is a healthy position for a Christian to take. But it could also be a way of shoving a complex problem into the category of "unsolvable" and dropping the issue.

A fourth position is that man is both determined and also has freedom to choose against his past, but the *degree of determinism and freedom varies* from person to person. A professional in mental health could say that the healthy

72

person has more potential freedom than the unhealthy and this varies on a continuum. The neurotic has more freedom than the psychotic, and the mentally healthy person more freedom than both. To phrase it another way, the more a man is motivated by his unconscious, the less freedom he has to choose against his past because he is less aware of the factors influencing him at any point. This appears to be a realistic view to those working with the emotionally disturbed.

A fifth view, which could possibly be assigned to one of the other views, is the *habit-freedom hypothesis*. This view proposes that man is determined by his past experiences but can depart from this pattern if he so chooses. Most people, however, do not choose to change the habit patterns and ways of thinking which their past has pressed upon them. Having become creatures of habit, they choose not to challenge the deterministic factors which dictate their behavior. They are therefore quite predictable until they decide to reevaluate their past and possibly choose another course of action. This, say some, is a picture of most humanity—victims of their culture and environment, choosing to respond passively to its pressure without a struggle. Although it may be a pathetic picture of humanity, it probably represents most of mankind.

Many Christians tend to identify with the existential position in regard to the problem of determinism, considering determinism a threat to the historic Christian position. I should like to suggest that determinism is not incompatible with a Biblical view of man. In my opinion, any of the above-mentioned theories within a deterministic framework could be maintained by a Christian, depending in part upon the theological framework in which he works. The most difficult position would be that of complete determinism, but it is possible even to believe this if one is strongly convinced of a theistic determinism based on God's sovereignty.

The determinism-freedom problem in some respects sounds like the predestination-freedom problem which has plagued the church for centuries. From my vantage point, to disregard the deterministic position is to alienate oneself

73

from the stream of intellectual investigation which has captured the minds of men and which marks much of the research in the social sciences. To suggest that determinism in the affairs of men is not a powerful factor is to ignore the mass of data the social scientists have amassed during the past five or six decades. The Christian must face the issue and consider the options.

BIBLIOGRAPHY

What, Then, Is Man? A Symposium of Theology, Psychology, and Psychiatry. St. Louis: Concordia Publishing House. 1958.

Tournier, Paul. *The Person Reborn*. New York: Harper & Row, Inc. 1966.

AS THE TWIG IS BENT
Ages 0-1

If a child does not perceive love in his primitive world, it will be difficult for him to conceive of anyone, man or God, loving him.

8

AS THE TWIG IS BENT

Ages 0-1—The Foundation of Personality

THE injunction of the Bible is, "Train up a child in the way he should go, and when he is old, he will not depart from it." A simple statement and a simple promise. But when we begin to break down the statement it changes from the simple to the very complex. What is "the way he should go"? Determining what we want the child to be is a terribly complex problem, and added to it is the problem of trying to bring this about in everyday living. How can we work this statement out in practice?

Some insights into the developmental process of young children can give us some guides along what seems like a familiar route but is in reality an uncharted course.

There is almost universal agreement among professionals in the field of child development that the first six years are the most important in any person's life. When a child enters the world he is completely dependent, uncoordinated, asocial. Often he is a frustrating human being to his parents. By the age of six the child is an individual who has

77

developed gross motor coordination to the extent that he can jump, walk, run, and make skillful bodily maneuvers. He has the fine motor coordination which enables him to take a pencil or crayon and with imagination draw, color, and perhaps even write his name.

The six-year-old child can interact with other children both in play and in serious work enterprises. He can play war, football, hopscotch, and simple card games, and can assemble complicated puzzles. He can control his angry impulses to such an extent that there is a minimum of danger to himself or other children. He is expected to sit in a classroom for five or six hours a day with a minimum of fidgeting, and he has the ability to respond appropriately to the demands of a teacher or a parent. He has a basic knowledge of what his parents and his friends think is right or wrong and can usually conduct himself according to these principles; i.e., he has the core of a conscience. He can handle complex symbols, language being the most obvious, and can communicate to almost everyone his needs, hopes, and fears. He also has learned the subtle communication of gesture, facial expression, and bodily postures.

Although the child has come this far from birth, he is not a paragon of virtue. Occasionally he hurts others, physically and verbally. He does not have complete mastery of his body, as is easily demonstrated by his awkward attempts to catch and throw a ball or his inability to draw complex designs. Yet, though he has obvious limitations, he has all the skills and abilities to function in both a child's and an adult's world. What he has learned during these first six years, he has learned well. If he is lacking in any area, especially his control over aggressive impulses, the parents will soon find this out when they have their first school conferences with the teacher.

The child has moved from an asocial being to a social being with excellent skills of communication. The road was rocky and the hurdles tough, but he has made it. He has been socialized. Is it any wonder that the first six years are so crucial?

As a psychologist, I want to point out some of the significant hurdles and developmental changes which occur and try to relate these to the child's religious concepts. We usually consider the developmental journey as beginning after the birth process without much concern over the birth experience itself. The mother knows of her ordeal of labor and adjustment with this infant, but what of the child? This child was a functioning organism months before the actual birth trauma; even if he were born several months prematurely he might possibly survive. The child is very much alive before birth and is a sensing, reacting human being. We can only speculate on what he feels or experiences during this time, but it is obvious that his world is one of warmth, pressure, fluid, and perhaps some noise. One can only imagine what the heartbeat or the gastric rumblings of his mother sound like to the baby, but it is highly probable that both can be heard. The heartbeat will naturally be associated with this warmth, fluid, confined, but rather comfortable existence. It has been demonstrated that the prenatal child is capable of simple learning such as responding reflexively to loud noises.

Then comes the change. The water dissipates; the child is put under immense pressure and forced from his comfortable world into a foreign environment. This is a world of lights, noise, cold, and freedom from restraint—freedom to manipulate his arms and legs and to cry. What the child feels as he is handled, washed, and held in the most undignified positions can only be guessed, but it probably can be summed up in the word "anxiety."

The newborn child is a functioning organism completely dependent upon others, just as he was before birth, but in some way he must now make order out of the chaos around him. He must adjust to acquiring his nourishment through sucking; he must learn to organize his sensory experiences. He must learn what is right side up, where noise comes from, and what he is and what he is not. He must learn that he is an entity separate from the world outside. He must develop a self-concept which demands much differentiation between his internal and external senses. He must distinguish himself from the bombarding of external stimuli. We enjoy watching a child observe his hands or play with his feet. Through these experiences he is discovering that they are in some way his and that he has control

79

over them. He is beginning to identify himself as separate and unique. His feet are different from the bed, the wall, his mother's breast, and he has some control over his appendages.

I concur with those who say that this first year of life is the most important year in a person's existence. During this year he learns whether the world is cruel or comfortable; he learns that he is a separate entity apart from the world of stimuli outside him. This year is the foundation on which all of personality rests, a foundation which is almost impossible to rebuild or repair because the memories and experiences are locked in and cannot be recalled except in a distorted, symbolic dream world or a vague undifferentiated feeling.

The person of major significance in this extremely important year is, obviously, the mother. She holds the child, feeds him, comforts him when in distress, warms him when cold. She holds him to her breast and feeds him and in so doing returns him periodically to a womblike condition of warmth and snug confinement. She rocks the child and gives him the awareness of motion which he often sensed before birth. It is she who protects the child from the traumas of life until he is able to handle life more readily. It is she who takes the child through the after-phases of the birth trauma to a semblance of autonomy, which occurs around the end of the first year. This grave responsibility is usually accomplished with much frustration, especially for the first child of a mother, but also with much care and affection.

For the woman who did not want a child, however, or the one who is preoccupied with herself and her own problems, the child becomes an added burden, an unwanted guest with fantastic demands. Such a woman is unable to give of herself to this utterly dependent person. It is this child who suffers, and who will find the foundation weak when the pressures of life increase during the maturing process. If the child comes through this period anxious, insecure, frustrated, these reactions will probably be a pattern for life. It has been documented again and again that children who are brought up in foundling homes or by

80

cold, detached mothers tend to be good candidates for mental health problems.

Responsible parents must see this first year as critical. The child is developing an emotional set about the world in which he is to live—a world of emotional experiences which will shape his attitude toward life and which will resist a reasonable judgment to the contrary at a later period.

What the child learns during this period of time is indelibly written into his life and will influence many of his later ideas and values, including his religious ones. He will have an emotive response to the world in general, and his ultimate hopes and fears will be rooted in the primitive awareness of the world as he has felt and experienced it. Is this world safe or threatening? The healthy child will be aware that the world is, at times, frightening; but he will have an overriding awareness that he is protected from most of the dangers of life.

If a child has been overprotected, he will not have the experiences which would caution him about the realistic thorns and sharp places of life. On the other hand, he must not be overwhelmed by hurt or rejection lest he withdraw and cringe from the painful experience called life. If the child is not cared for and is buffeted back and forth from home to home, rejected, unhandled, uncuddled, unloved, this child will chronically feel the pain of insecurity and the constant fear of pain. This child has the stage prepared for a history of severe mental health maladjustments. The case files and research data from foundling homes overwhelmingly support the fact that children deprived of care and love, who are rejected during this period, make poor adjustments to life and are more likely to have interpersonal maladjustments.

During this first year, basic trust in people develops, especially trust in the "big people." Do these people love, and can they give of this love? Love is communicated in many ways: the way a child is held, the way the mother talks to the baby, the way she responds to a cry of discomfort, the way she holds the baby close to her while feeding; the father's smile, laughter, and concern. The whisper of quietness, the upheavals of play, all are important in this child's developing concept of basic trust.

The memories of these experiences are only vague feelings, illusive impressions, an indescribable awareness of security or lack of it—feelings which will carry over into all interpersonal relationships and eventually into the growing child's concept of God. I have seen children hurt so often by people that the dog or cat in the house becomes the only thing they can trust. As the child learns about God he may respond to God as he would to any of the "big people" in his life. He may readily trust this God because "big people" are trustworthy, or he may cringe in fear when God is characterized in human terms because "big people" have hurt him.

Love, like trust, is illusive, but the child knows whether it is there or not. If the parents communicate love, the child will have little difficulty believing and trusting the fact that God also can love just as Mother and Father do. If he does not perceive love in his primitive world, it will be difficult for him to conceive of anyone, man or God, loving him.

The child's self-concept certainly will reflect his parents' attitudes toward him. If a child is loved, he conceives of himself as being of worth and value; he feels important and significant. The child who knows only rejection and lack of love thinks of himself as unlovable and worthless. If a person believes he is unlovable, he not only thinks of himself as unworthy of human love but he is unable to understand that God loves him.

In this first, most important year in the life of the developing person, much has occurred which will influence him for the rest of his life. Yet this early impression may be offset somewhat by later developmental experiences. Even in the poorest of homes the parents are able to give love and some security to the child, and this may be enough to help him move on and establish a fairly healthy existence. Even the best of parents reject the child at times because he is demanding and interferes with their lives and personal interests. Even the healthiest of homes have friction and confusion which the child senses.

It is believed that the cause of many severe disturbances

in both children and adults can be placed in this first year of development. For the child who suffers much, the die may be cast for chronic maladjustment to life. Loved or rejected—the child is started on "the way he should go."

AS THE TWIG IS BENT
Ages 1-3

Is God basically a rule-giver and enforcer, or does He encourage personal development and exploration? What we think about God is often closely related to what we think about our parents.

9

AS THE TWIG IS BENT

Ages 1-3—The Age of Negativism

ABOUT the age of one, this cute little baby becomes quite "independent." His developing ability to crawl and walk enables him to get into more trouble.

By this time he usually is weaned and is less and less dependent on the presence of his mother to gain nourishment, as he is beginning to feed himself. The other members of the family take larger places of prominence in his life. He can interact with his father in play or warm affectionate behavior. His brothers and sisters become more and more important, as their frustrations and jealousies begin to take on actual physical proportions. The brother's toy is grabbed out of the child's hand, he is isolated from the sister's game with her friends or is ushered unceremoniously out of the brother's room. These other children are actively competing for the mother's attention, and are more likely to gain it since the infant has become less and less dependent on her, freeing her to give more time to the other children.

In general one might say that by his first birthday the

child's umbilical cord is broken, or should be. The child should be entering a new phase of development, a period of socialization. Traumatic as this period may be for child and parent, the years from one to three are critical for adequate future functioning. The child must learn that the world is not all love and play; it is also a world of rules and relationships. The rules must be understood and obeyed, and the relationships must be evaluated with more and more appropriate responses. The child must ask such questions as: How do I respond to the "big people"? What can I do or not do? What will be the consequences if I do not obey the rules? What will the "big people" do to me if I disobey? Will they actually spank me if I climb on the neighbor's coffee table?

During this time the parents become very frustrated. This is especially true of the mother. If she sets up many rules and tries to enforce them, she plays the role of the house "ogre" and finds herself always redirecting the child by command or shout. She may have to back up her instructions with repeated warnings or actual physical violence. Even a mother who is convinced that redirection rather than punishment is the best way of shaping the child's life often resorts to a healthy shout or a swat on the bottom to relieve frustration and get the child to perform the way she wants.

The child's task is to learn the rules of the game and to test them to see if the rule-makers will enforce them. The task often takes the form of a parent-child struggle of great magnitude. In technical language this period is called an age of negativism, a time when the child occasionally disobeys to see whether the rules will be enforced and when he tries to assert his developing awareness of personal autonomy. His budding awareness that he is really an individual and has some control over his interests and experiences will be very important to him during this period.

The parents, on the other hand, want this child to function in a world that has many thorns without getting severely hurt, either psychologically or physically. They do not want him to put his fingers in an electric socket, run out into the street, or be rejected for antisocial behavior. They do not want him to destroy property, nor do they want to crush his curiosity. They want him to enjoy life, but they want him to fit into the family structure. They want him to be loved by his brothers and sisters and to return this love, and they want to keep jealousy and rivalry to a minimum. They want to make this egocentric human being into a person who is other centered—one who thinks of the welfare of others while considering his own needs and aspirations. It is superfluous to tell parents with a child in this stage that the process of socialization is exacting and very frustrating. They know it through many vivid, exasperating experiences.

Often the parent, usually the mother (although fathers often join the club), feels terribly guilty for continually yelling and thwarting the child during the day. It often seems to many mothers that their days are filled with such comments as "stop it," "get off the table," "go away," "come back here." If a kind word is spoken, it is only in a moment of exhaustion or in response to the child's smile or creative effort; but the general impact of the day is one of conflict, control, and frustration. It is not unusual to find a parent falling into a chair at the end of a day in a state of exhaustion, feeling very guilty for being such a "poor" parent. This feeling is quite normal for the average parent and should be accepted as such.

The socialization process is hard for parent and child. But guilt feelings may be productive, encouraging the parent to seek more creative ways of helping the child to more positive efforts; or they may force the mother to let up and allow the child freedom, freedom tomorrow where he had none today. This is not necessarily bad if one has been too strict. But changing the rules does create a problem. Yesterday the child could not sit on the coffee table; today he can. Changing the rules of the game frustrates the child. He may imagine that all the rules of the game of living are subject to change, and therefore be encouraged to test them all.

Vacillating parents, often motivated by guilt or personal insecurity, tend to produce children who are hard to control, insecure, and who reject the authority of adults. This type of parent may also produce a very anxious child, especially if they give severe punishment for disobedience. The child never knows when the blow will come. If the rules are not clear, the child is never sure what is right and lives in a state of confusion. Such a situation forces the child to become an excellent evaluator of parental moods. If he sees that the parent is gay and easygoing, it may mean that the door is open, go ahead; but if the parent is depressed and self-preoccupied, it may mean to keep out of trouble. A child who must become an expert in manipulating parents by recognizing their emotional state is very demanding and frustrating.

The keys to the socialization process are consistency and parental goals. Are the rules well thought through and consistent with parental long-range goals; or are they spur-of-the-moment decisions, subject to frequent change? There are many homes where the communication between parents is poor and the methods of child-rearing are not agreed upon. One parent is stern and the other permissive, each going to the extreme to compensate for the other's overindulgence or strictness. The child is always the loser because he learns two sets of rules and vacillates back and forth between them, depending upon who is present and who has the most power. The child ends up as a master manipulator of adults and often terribly frustrated.

During this stage the child is also developing as a person. He becomes aware of his own impulses and needs. His fantasies during this period are crucial to our understanding him. He has ambivalent feelings about his parents: he obviously needs them and returns the affection they have for him; on the other hand, he becomes very angry when they frustrate many of his attempts to be inquisitive and independent, and when they punish his antisocial behavior.

The child is told not to throw sand at the neighbor's child and is punished when he does. The rule and the punishment cause personal hostility toward the parent and yet are sources of security to the child. He is angry because he has been frustrated, but he also knows that when his anger gets out of hand, an adult will step in and help him control it. The child, therefore, loves and hates his parents.

The child is seldom allowed to express his frustration and anger, but is usually encouraged to express love and affection. But anger does not just dissipate with time; it is channeled into many other areas—aggressive behavior with other children, aggressive play with toys, and, often, aggressive fantasies. Here is the value of a child's vicarious psychological experiences from the reading of fairy tales or the watching of TV cartoons. In the fairy tales the little animals or children get away from or destroy the big animals or witch (a perfect bad-mother symbol). On TV the little mouse pulverizes the big cat (parent figure) and becomes the local hero. These stories appeal to children because they match their fantasies and help them to express their pent-up angry feelings. Fairy tales or cartoons thus can be very therapeutic to the developing child.

A child's fantasy life is full of aggressive themes which he acts out or vicariously enjoys. In his fantasy he can kill the giant one moment and hit his parents the next. I recall the verbalized fantasy of an anxious little boy after I had told him to stop doing something. He responded by saying that he would throw a book through my window and splatter glass all over my house. I assured him that if he tried somebody would be there to stop him. I was not worried, and he didn't have to be afraid lest it come true. This exchange illustrates the problem: if a child is given too much freedom he may become quite anxious lest he actually do what he fantasies. Since children do not have built-in controls, they must depend upon adults to provide the controls if their fragile controls do not work. A child knows that he could never act out his fantasies because a big person would stop him. If he felt that no control was available or that he could control adults he would become very anxious. He would fear that his fantasies might become reality: i.e., that he might hurt or kill the people who frustrate him.

I once had a very anxious seven-year-old boy in therapy. We discovered that his mother did whatever he wished so that, in essence, he had control over her. He had frightening delusions of omnipotence—a little boy controlling one of the "big people." He was also anxious because he was literally afraid that he would do what he fantasized, because if he could control the "big people" who should control him, who would stop him? After some extended counseling with the mother, she was able to cut down his anxiety considerably by letting the child know that she was boss. He learned that he need not fear his fantasies because either she or some other "big person" would stop him if he began to get out of control. Children must know that "big people" can control little children; that is one of the prime rules of the socialization process. Usually this is communicated adequately, and the child's fantasies are not terribly frustrating to him.

The struggle for autonomy and the relationship to the adult world seem to focus on two areas. One is the toilet training process and the other is eating. In both situations the child has obvious command if he decides to have it. He can control his bowels and urination as he so wills; and he can eat or not eat as he so wills. This negativistic period is often made forcefully clear when the child resists the insertion of a spoon into his mouth during mealtime. In fact, the times of general resistance to almost any parental instruction become a point of exasperation in the parents' lives.

It is important, however, for the child's developing self-concept that he experience autonomy. He should occasionally be able to stand up to parental demands; but if he wins too often, he ultimately loses out to anxiety. If, on the other hand, he is always forced to capitulate, his spirit and struggle for personal autonomy can be crushed. Occasionally one meets a child who is hyperobedient, passive, and fearful of adults. This child's spirit has been broken by the strong pressures from the "big people."

There are two good principles for handling children in this period. (1) Have few rules and enforce them consistently. (2) Try to understand that in asserting autonomy the child is not trying to hurt the parent; this is simply his attempt to find out what the rules are and who he is in relationship to adults. This self-discovering child needs firm controls, yet as much freedom as possible, to discover who he is and what kind of world he lives in.

The developing child is beginning to form crude and primitive concepts about religion and God. I asked my three-year-old daughter what she thought God was like. She was not sure what to say, but she did inform me that "she lives

92

in the church." Her Sunday school teacher who cares for her on Sunday morning had become the concrete God-figure for her. Children at this age cannot think abstractly; therefore everything must be concretized for them.

To tell a child that God is strong like Dad or loving like Mother tells him something he can understand. To say that God is everywhere, like the wind, or that God is seen best in Jesus Christ is to make the abstract meaningful. These early impressions become permanently tucked away in the child's thought processes; when he becomes an adult this residue of early associations will be recalled.

The obvious danger in the attempt to make an abstract concept concrete is that extraneous elements are added. To say that God is like a father may mean much more to the child than that God is strong and the provider of the family. It may mean that God is also stern, unapproachable, and punitive. The church may sometimes foster these inappropriate associations. A Sunday school teacher who admonishes a child to obey his parents because it pleases God may be reinforcing the parent-God model. The parental rules may be taken as God's rules, and the child's ambivalent attitude toward parental rules may carry over to God and "his rules." Some parents strengthen the association by informing the child that God will not like it if he disobeys his parents' wishes. Many parents who do this are too inadequate to enforce their rules; so they use God as the "omnipotent switch" to back them up. In so doing, they direct the child's anger and frustration toward God, who is perceived as an all-powerful lawgiver who sides with parents.

It would be much healthier for the child to be angry with the parents than with a vague, amorphous God. Childish anger with parents can be understood and dealt with, but when the anger becomes God-directed, it is less easy to handle and may have eternal consequences. Not infrequently, these childhood feelings are expressed when a child begins to become independent of his parents during adolescence. The adolescent may reject his parent-like God in his rejection of his parents. When one sees this one wonders how the Biblical God ever can become a living reality to persons who associate parents with God.

This period of socialization is the period of the most

basic and yet most primitive thought patterns about God. Is God punitive and overwhelming, or is he compassionate and considerate? Is he to be feared or trusted? Will he crush self-assertion or will he be gentle and encourage self-expression? Is he interested more in the person or in the way a person behaves? Is God basically a rule-giver and enforcer or does he encourage personal development and exploration? The concept of God is often closely related to how a child sees his parents. It is a monumental task for both parents and the church to reduce parental-God associations which would deform and misrepresent the Biblical concept of God.

AS THE TWIG IS BENT
Ages 3-6

The child, and probably on an unconscious level the adult also, may react in part to the Christian Trinity as a symbolic representation of his own struggles for an identity. The natural propensity to be hostile towards the father as a competitor for the mother's affections may be reflected in . . . unconscious attitudes toward God the Father.

10.

AS THE TWIG IS BENT

Ages 3-6—The Age of Identification

How does a boy differ from a girl? The answer at first glance seems obvious and a little ridiculous. When the question is thought through, however, the answer becomes quite complex.

If we would list the various patterns of behavior which a boy or girl is expected to perform, we can begin to realize that what a boy or girl does is largely determined by parental and cultural expectations. If we were to ask several parents what a boy should be like in terms of his behavior, we might be very surprised at the variety of responses. One parent might want a boy who was rough and tumble, interested in football, liked to wrestle with his father and to play war games. Another parent might want a boy interested in art, music, and reading. In most instances the child will meet the parents' expectations unless there is conflict in the home; in that case the child has to choose one parental expectation over the other.

Just how the child is molded into parental expectations of his particular sex role is complex but not very difficult to understand. The major method is *identification*. In the identification process the child is encouraged to be like one of the parents, who becomes the model. In most homes the model for the boy is the father and the model for the girl is the mother.

We may find the typical girl thumping around in her mother's high-heeled shoes and wearing her mother's dresses, which drag behind her like a wedding train. She cooks an imaginary meal in a play oven, irons some clothes on a play ironing board with a toy iron, and changes the diaper on her doll. A typical girl—yes, and one who is obviously in the process of becoming like her mother. She is playing the game of mothering, and this will be helpful in her later life when she becomes like her mother in reality. She is becoming closely identified with her sex role through social imitation and social encouragement.

This little girl is given many reinforcements for being like "mommy." When she bakes something in her play oven everyone smiles, eats a little, chokes a little, and praises the child for her work and, indirectly, for her feminine interests. When she dresses up to go out, everyone tells her how nice she looks and that she is a cute *girl*, thus encouraging her interest in clothes, prettiness, and other feminine roles.

It is considered quite unusual for a boy to be interested in dolls, ironing, cooking, and wearing frilly clothes. Most boys are not encouraged in behavior patterns which are culturally feminine, but if they were, they would be just as concerned with playing house and cooking as any girl. The fact is that boys are encouraged to play catch, wrestle with other boys, make things from wood, and go fishing, thus setting the scene for a masculine identification. They are actually discouraged from becoming interested in playing dolls and dressing up. The role expectations for boys and girls are quite different and are usually very clear to them—although the roles are not as clearly differentiated now as they were a few decades ago.

The important factor in this role identification is the presence of a model who is not too threatening. The fact that the mother is almost always present during the first six years of a child's life, and is usually more approachable than the father, makes it easy for the girl to identify with her mother. There are, of course, exceptions; a girl could identify with her father and assume a more aggressive, businesslike role in life. Such a girl might be as much interested in football as in dressmaking and might be more interested in a profession than in keeping house.

Although girls occasionally identify with their fathers, the problem is that boys find it easier to identify with their mothers than with their fathers. The mother is around the home much more than the father, and if the mother needs to have the boy emulate her, the problem rapidly becomes monumental. The father sees his son only in the evening and on weekends. If he does not go out of his way to encourage a close relationship with his son, the boy may have no alternative but to identify with the major source of security and affection, his mother. A father who is very busy trying to develop himself professionally or for some reason prefers not to spend much time at home, makes it very difficult for the son to identify with him. To compound the problem, when the boy goes to school he is usually given women teachers at least through grade school.

During the ages of three to six the nucleus of basic identification takes place. The child becomes quite aware of basic physical sex differences, and this difference is reinforced by a variety of social pressures, especially parental and peer. The boy who is interested in dolls, hopscotch, and looking at books is quickly isolated from the other boys in the neighborhood. The girl who prefers to play catch and to climb trees with the boys is considered by her peer group as strange.

The process of discovering the basic sex differences, either socially or physically, is not always easy. During this stage of development children often play the game of "doctors and nurses." Even though it is an interesting social game, not infrequently it develops into a game of inspection and discovery of sexual and individual differences. To find that the "doctor" boy next door has a physical protrusion and that the "nurse" girl does not is indeed interesting and at times very confusing. When children learn that this is the main physical difference between boys and girls they will ask why. Some girls have fantasies that for some reason they have been cheated because they have not been given what the boys have. Some boys fear that if they are not careful they will lose what they have and become like girls. Some girls even fear that they have been castrated.

If parents understand that one of the prime concerns of a child during this period is his interest in discovering his sexual identity, they will understand and encourage his self-discovery in a socially healthy way. When parents walk into an involved game of doctor and nurse to find their children with their pants off or over in a corner exploring one another, their first impulse is to project onto these children all types of sexual adult fantasies which are often far from the childrens' interests. The children are concerned more with sexual investigation than with sexual stimulation, although this is not always the case. The parents' usual reaction is to order the children to put their clothes back on, warn them never to do this again, and at the same time resist giving evidence of the shock they have just sustained. Then the parents go off and rationalize the problem, finally deciding that it is the neighbor child who is "oversexed" and therefore the instigator. It is far better to realize, however, that this curiosity is common to all children; it should not be categorically condemned but should be satisfied through more socially acceptable means. These include books, museums, animals, and open discussion in the family of the differences between men and women when confronted with questions or with the nakedness of parents or peers.

Freud and other psychoanalysts have pointed out one of the difficult problems which must be resolved during this stage: the fact that boys develop a strong interest in the mother and the girls a strong interest in the father. The desire for the boy to take his father's place and for the girl to take her mother's place not only draws them closer to the parent of the opposite sex but also tends to cause some strain and resentment toward the parent of the same sex. The parent who needs and enjoys this special attention by the child of the opposite sex may indulge himself or herself and in so doing will make the sex role identification process harder for the child. The boy will tend to spend more and more time with the mother and the girl more and more time with the father, reducing the amount of closeness to the parent with whom the child should identify. The child must love and lose. The child must learn that he can never take the place of the parent of the same sex. He should be encouraged to be like the parent of the same sex and to help solidify that relationship.

An example of extreme sex identification confusion are the "Don Juans" who need to prove their masculinity, or the homosexuals who have identified so strongly with persons of the opposite sex that their sexual fantasies are like those of the opposite sex. I remember counseling a young man who was having homosexual preoccupations. His mother and father were incompatible but continued to live together. In her desperate need to be loved the mother allowed this boy to meet her needs and encouraged this identification with her. He became her source of affection and in many ways, by vicariously living through him, she made him her alter-ego. In the process of identification he became like her in behavior and thought.

The psychoanalytic writers have drawn attention to the sexual overtones of religious concepts. In the sexual identity struggle the relationships within the family triad are most crucial. What a young boy thinks of his mother and father may have some carryover into his religious ideas. The Trinity can be taken as a picture of this same triad—God the Father, Christ the Son, and the Holy Spirit as the feminine member. The parallel relationship becomes more obvious in Roman Catholicism which not only stresses the Father and the Son, but also Mary, an obvious symbol of mother. The child, and probably on an unconscious level the adult also, may react in part to the Christian Trinity as a symbolic representation of his own struggles for an identity. The natural propensity to be hostile towards the father as a competitor for the mother's affections may be reflected in his unconscious attitudes toward God the Father. This competitiveness for the mother and hostility towards the father may also produce conscious and unconscious guilt feelings which may compound the emotive response to the male or female components of a trinity. To tell children

101

that God is asexual or a unity may resolve the problem theologically, but it does not handle the issue psychologically. God is still discussed using the pronoun "He," nor can Christ's masculinity be casually overlooked.

A girl may have less problems in responding to a masculine God figure because she has had for years a natural affection for her father and a deep-seated interest in pleasing him. When this is projected into a religious context the girl or woman can have more positive emotion towards God. In Christianity it appears that women have more fervent religious emotion and participate more in church programs than do men, and one can only suspect that the masculine Christian Deity may be one of the main reasons for the apparent religious emotional discrepancy between men and women.

Just what a person thinks consciously or unconsciously when he is asked to love Christ is hard to evaluate. The concept will vary from person to person, but it may not be void of sexual overtones. When the Catholic nun marries Christ and the Church and wears a ring to represent this heavenly marriage, one sees how obviously there is some sexual residue. What does a young woman think or feel when she is asked to love Christ and give everything to him? What goes through the consciousness and unconsciousness of a young man who is struggling for a sexual identity and is overtly encouraged to love Christ, a male figure? It is not easy to desexualize these religious symbols and to take them from the concrete into the world of the abstract.

Of the parents, the mother tends to be more approachable and understanding; the father, on the other hand, is usually harsher, more distant, and less empathetic. Because of this, a masculine God-concept may inhibit some people because God is also seen as punitive, distant, and nonempathetic. A feminine God-concept would, for many people, be easier to appreciate psychologically because this God would be more understanding and approachable. The Roman Catholic church, by placing Mary as the mediatrix, has introduced a strong feminine element into the God-concept making it psychologically easier for some to comprehend and accept the Christian God. To have the mother

102

intercede on behalf of her child to the father is psychologically solid in light of the reality of the developing child's experience.

How the church should begin to handle this problem is difficult to say, but to be aware of the problem is certainly the first and probably the most important step. Teachers and leaders might be more careful in addressing God in prayer as "Father," taking into account, if possible, what kind of fathers the persons present have. They should recognize that calling God "Father" may only produce anxiety or hostility in some hearers rather than positive emotions. Pointing to Christ as God incarnate may reduce many of the parent-child conflicts; Christ is seen psychologically more as a companion or older brother. Another suggestion is to revitalize the Old Testament concept of God which emphasizes the sexual unity of God—the union in God of both masculine and feminine elements. This may be seen from the account of man's creation. "God created man in his own image . . . male and female created he them" (Genesis 1:27. See also Proverbs 8). God is pictured as having both fatherly and motherly attributes. He loves his people not only like a father, but also like a mother (Isaiah 49:15, and elsewhere).

AS THE TWIG IS BENT
Adolescence

[Adolescents] may even throw out Christianity as a legitimate option because of the gross inconsistencies which the adult world displays. Such adolescents have much to offer the Christian community as they struggle for personal meaning, virtue, and self-identity.

11

AS THE TWIG IS BENT

Adolescence—A Period of Rebirth

THE adolescent is infamous for many things, not the least of which is his tendency to abandon his religious heritage. He tends to lose interest in the church and seems to challenge the values and life styles which the church and the adult world appear to cherish. The adult world, and often the adolescents themselves, are often quite perplexed and confused as they move through this period.

The turmoils of adolescence are frustrating for both the adolescent and the adult. The adolescent appears chronically inconsistent. He asserts that he wants to see virtue triumph, yet he cheats on exams. He rejects the crass materialism of the adult world, yet is caught "drooling" over a new Honda in the shop window. At one moment he is a source of boundless energy; but when this energy needs to be channeled in creative work, he appears completely depleted of all energy and barely able to stagger around.

This bundle of inconsistency may give of himself to a worthy social cause but in the same day ostracize someone who does not fit into his clique. This human being spends much of his time clamoring for friendships, but he may also cloister himself in his room, withdrawing from the source of companionship. At one moment he is gay and full of laughter; the next he is depressed and moody. The adolescent rejects authority yet worships idols of his choice without reservation. This is the normal adolescent, a source of wonder and confusion to himself and to adults.

This maturing person has some problems of great magnitude which he must resolve. First, he must begin to establish some form of autonomy from his parents. The ease of this task depends in large measure upon the parents. If the parents encourage autonomy, and yet give some support when it is needed through these years, the process will be fairly painless. But if the parents demand unquestioning obedience to their way of life, the child will have but two courses open to him. One is to openly revolt, and the other is to retreat passively from autonomous strivings. In each case the hostility and resentment will run high; only in one case the anger is expressed and in the other it is repressed.

The process of obtaining a major degree of independence is difficult for many adolescents. Even when they are given autonomy by parents, what frequently happens is that one source of dependence is substituted for another. The adolescent rejects the control and support of his parents but finds support and protection in his unquestioned allegiance to his peer group. This group has its own set of values, mores, and methods of social sanction. A child who is not accepted into this peer world has little source of security apart from the parents and will be reluctant to break away from the stability, and consequently the value controls, of the parents. Adolescents crave support in their struggle for independence and usually find it in the peer group.

I have observed a number of students who have been forced, by much pressure from home, to delay the overt expression of their strivings for independence until they could get away from home and go to college. At college, the volcano which has been building for a number of years often breaks loose, and any authority figure who comes in contact with the student feels the indiscriminate anger which had been suppressed for a number of years. Any authority figure, teacher or college administrator, becomes a

108

person to challenge and criticize just because he symbolizes parental figures.

The second major hurdle during this period is the necessary adjustment to the powerful new sexual drive which the maturing person finds, at times, overwhelming. Erik Erikson calls this a period of "physiological revolution"—a period when the entire body undergoes a rapid metamorphosis and young persons must learn to think of themselves in different terms. They grow taller, their body proportions change, physical sexual development becomes obvious, clothes do not fit, and they begin to worry about their adult physical features. When they compare their features with their models—movie stars, athletes, celebrities of all types—they begin to worry about their own inadequacies. The girl may wonder if she will be sought after because she is too tall or her breasts are not large enough. The boy may worry that he will not be tall enough to be taken seriously as a date, or that he will not be strong enough to assert himself in competitive sports.

The guilt and fear which parallel the sexual development can ultimately cripple the growing young person. What does he do with the sex drive? He can repress the drive and force it from consciousness; but this is done at great sacrifice to his entire psychic functioning. He can express it in the natural action of sexual intercourse, as some do; but the social stigma, ingrained values, potential fear of childbirth, and guilt may reduce this as a possibility. The main outlet of sexual expression for most young men is masturbation—the common, but seldom talked about, procedure for relieving sexual tension by oneself. If Kinsey's report is anywhere near accurate, it is a way of life for most unmarried males, and is also common among females. The major problem with this method of handling the sex drive is the guilt feelings which usually parallel the act. For many young people this behavior is almost synonymous with the unpardonable sin.

It is fairly reasonable to see why sex behavior, of all behavior, appears to carry the biggest burden of guilt. It is obvious that if either sex or aggression is not carefully controlled through the socialization process, our civilization as it is now constituted will not be able to stand. Therefore, sex—a normal, healthy, human and animal impulse—must be controlled through the socialization process. As we have seen, this process begins quite early and is continually reinforced. How does the mother or father respond when the young child begins to manipulate the genitals? What happens when the infant toddles into a room full of guests, minus his clothes? What happens when the four-year-old is found exploring the neighbor child's exposed "bottom"? Why does the stork get into the picture of childbirth? Why does the preacher not talk about the prostitute and sexual intercourse? Is it because sex is so very bad that it must not be mentioned in public, or is this a verbal evasion which communicates (silently) that persons who engage in sexual intercourse outside of marriage are put in the worst category of all—"immoral"? What is on the minds of most parents when they push for an active youth program at church? Is it not that what most people want out of youth directors is a program which will keep the youth active . . . and ipso facto out of the bushes?

It is generally conceded that the healthiest way of controlling the sexual drive is to sublimate it through healthy creative work and play. This is easy to say but hard to carry out. How does a conscientious student, who spends hours in school and in studying, find outlets through which to channel his energy? Although sublimation is the ideal, it appears inadequate in many people's lives and one of the previously mentioned outlets for sexual expression is usual.

The church should be understanding of the dilemma of most adolescents. Instead of increasing guilt feelings in an attempt at control, the church should be a place of understanding and forgiveness, a place where healthy attitudes toward sex can be discovered. Guilt can control the sex impulses to some degree, but when sex standards are violated, the self-incriminations and self-punishment can be intense. Tournier, in his perceptive volume *A Doctor's Casebook in Light of the Bible,* says: "In the privacy of my consulting-room men and women of all ages have often told me that they believe in God's forgiveness for any sin except their sexual ones. For such sins they feel God can never forgive them, but only despise them forever" (p. 62).

It is the responsibility of the church to put sex in its

rightful place—a natural human instinct which must be socialized for the maintenance of society and as an expression of oneness in the love relationship. It should be pointed out by practice and precept that a violation of one's sex values should be no more reprehensible than to defame a person through vengeful gossip.

The adolescent must begin not only the painful process of separation from his parents, the task of adapting to the developing sex drive and of accepting his own body as it develops, but he must also discover a personal identity which is uniquely himself. He must find his own values and his own ability level. He must begin to understand what motivates him. He must learn to discriminate between what his parents and peers say about him and what he says about himself. This is a very difficult process, for the pressures to conform to either parents or peer groups are immense. Before this adolescent can become an independent, productive person he must find himself within the myriad pressures which would mold him to conform to the values of others. In a sense one might say that this developing person has need for a rebirth, a new look at himself. He must break out of the cocoon of imposed pressures and become himself as judged by himself.

It is well known that the adolescent is an idealist, tending to see the world in terms of black or white, good or evil. He is also looking for a cause which will give him something into which he can throw his boundless energy. Furthermore, he is looking for a source of stability outside the home which can support him through the adolescent period. For these reasons he is susceptible to appeals from causes which give him support, meaning, and an outlet for his altruism. From our studies of Christian conversion records we also learn that the adolescent is susceptible to an appeal to Christianity, since the major portion of conversions to Christianity occur during the adolescent years. It should be emphasized that young people are looking for anything which will supply emotional support and give personal meaning. They could just as well be converted to communism or any other social movement as to Christianity.

Many Christian parents become quite concerned when

111

their adolescent child begins to challenge the religious values which the parents hold sacred. This is in part healthy and often inevitable. The adolescent is trying to find out why people believe what they believe so that he can determine what he wants to believe as an individual. Adolescents want to relate what the pastor says in his sermons to reality, and, if it does not work, to discard it. They want to know how a person can claim to be a follower of Christ and yet be so unlike Christ.

To accept something without mature reflection is a doubtful practice for anyone, and the adolescent is becoming aware of this fact. He is especially sensitive concerning religious values because these are closely tied to parental expectations, discipline, and way of life. Almost anything that is derived from parental authority will be suspect by the adolescent just because he is in the process of separating himself from parental controls. Since girls in our culture are expected to continue under parental rule longer than boys, their questioning and adolescent reevaluation probably takes place later than in the case of the male adolescent.

Most churches find that some of their most zealous and hard-working members are the adolescents. They also are the ones who frequently point out the inconsistencies in the adult value system. To build big churches, drive big automobiles, and live in big beautiful homes, appears incongruous to youth who are very sensitive to the poor across town and to a world dying from spiritual and physical starvation. The adults' crass materialism is pointed out for what it is, and the youth shake their fingers and heads. They are repulsed by the display and find it inconsistent with the Christian ethic. They may even throw out Christianity as a legitimate option because of the gross inconsistencies which the adult world displays. Such adolescents have much to offer the Christian community as they struggle for personal meaning, virtue, and self-identity.

Adolescents are looking for persons who are not "adult-like" with whom they can identify during this transition period. They identify often with a teacher or a youth worker who is able to see the world as they see it, one who does not identify completely with the adult, parentlike world.

The most meaningful appeal to them is to conceive of God as a friend rather than as a dictatorial parent. They are psychologically prepared to accept Christ the companion who understands and who is with them through victory or failure. A God who loves them unconditionally, even though they make some serious misjudgments in the growing-up process, this is the God to whom they can respond. He is the God of I John 1:9 who accepts, forgives, and challenges them to mutual respect and personal virtue. If adolescents conceive of God as parentlike or chronically judgmental and punitive, they are likely to cower in fear or to revolt in great violence. The companion Christ of Matthew 28:20 and John 10:10 is the Christ of the adolescent.

BIBLIOGRAPHY

Tournier, Paul. *A Doctor's Casebook in the Light of the Bible.* New York: Harper & Row, Inc., 1960.

AS THE TWIG IS BENT
The College Years

Perhaps it could be said of the college student that he is not all sugar and spice nor all puppy-dog tails; he is a real person in a struggle to find himself in a complex and often frightening world of ideas, values, and change.

12.

AS THE TWIG IS BENT

The College Years—

A Period of Identity Crises

WHAT is today's college student like? Systematic research has attempted to discover data which will describe the student. Yet, even though we do have some statistical norms describing the average college student, when we discuss an individual student, we generally find him to be the exception. Most people have observations and theories which they believe will help to describe this illusive creature. Yet, because of interaction with a selective group of students, or from selective perception, the hypotheses made about the majority of students may be incorrect. This can be true even though one has spent many years working with them. Perhaps it is like the husband who has lived with his wife for many years but in a moment of crisis finds that he really does not know her and that now he needs to take a new look at the woman with whom he has been living.

In this chapter I shall try to give a brief summary of the

many studies made of college students and to present some insights from psychology. Reviewing these studies is like looking in a kaleidoscope; each new approach presents a slightly different picture, and one is left with only a vague impression of form and design. Much of the research has methodological flaws; it has been done with inadequate measuring instruments, and partakes of the limitations of the cross-sectional approach. Since there have been few comprehensive studies, the conclusions must be partial and suggestive rather than definitive. The best summary of the studies is the one by Wester, Freedman, and Heist,[1] summarizing Jacob's conclusions found in his book *Changing Values in College:*

> The student generation are "gloriously contented" in their present activity and in their outlook toward the future. They are "unabashedly self centered", aspiring above all to material gratifications for themselves and their families. Though conventionally middle-class they have an "easy tolerance of diversity" and are ready to live in a society without racial, ethnic, or income barriers. The traditional moral virtues, such as sincerity, honesty, and loyalty are highly valued, but there is little inclination to censor laxity, which students consider to be widespread. A need for religion is generally recognized, but students do not expect religious beliefs to govern daily decisions. Rather they expect that these decisions will be socially determined. The general tendency is to be "dutifully responsive toward government" but there is little inclination to contribute voluntarily to the public welfare or to seek an influential role in public affairs. "Students by and large set great stock in college in general and in their own college in particular", vocational preparation and skills and experience in social relations being regarded as the greatest benefits of college education.

A reading of the literature on the college student makes it obvious that both colleges and individuals may vary dras-

[1] In N. Sanford, ed., *The American College*, pp. 824–825.

tically from this general profile. In particular, this pattern may be very different from the pattern of students in Christian colleges because of the special admission standards and because of the Christian school's reputation which has an appeal to a rather well-defined constituency.

It is important to go beyond the statistical studies of the college student and take a look at him in depth. I think Erik Erikson has captured the essence of this age of growth in his concept of "identity crisis." He means by *identity* the "feeling of being at home in one's body, a sense of knowing where one is going, and an inner assurance of anticipated recognition from those who count."[2] In essence, the college period is a time for self-discovery, when parental evaluations of the student can be investigated and parental values reviewed and judged. Erikson claims that, for this evaluation, the young person must be separated from his parents and a period of neutrality, a "psychosocial moratorium," declared until the student can develop a synthesis of ideas, values, and behavior which are uniquely his own. During this period, superimposed values from home are frequently cast off and there is only minimum genuine commitment.

In the process of developing a self-concept with which a person can live with a minimum of conflict, there should be at least some physical independence from the parents. Even though this process of self-discovery begins early in life, it seems to come to focus during the college years, especially if the young adult can be separated from home pressures.

In our society the college is frequently seen as an extension of the home, but this situation varies from college to college. Some colleges assume little of the parental role, while others take right up where the home left off. Some Christian colleges obviously assume a strong parental role with its social regulations, a well-defined theological position, and implicit standards of expected moral and religious behavior. The stronger the control a college assumes over a student, the more it resembles the parents from whom the student is striving to be independent. As a natural consequence the student will express rebellion and hostility toward the institution because of his thwarted independence striv-

[2] "Identity and the Life Cycle," pp. 118–119.

ings. Some students do not enter this stage of self-discovery and exploration, but assume the same passive-submissive role to the college as they did to their parents. Some have an identity crisis as a delayed stage of development after college, and some never reevaluate themselves in light of a broader perspective.

A major characteristic of the adolescent in his strivings for independence is the way he vacillates in his relation to authority. He wants to be free from his parents and authority, and struggles to get out from under their control. At the same time he is not sure of his own impulse controls, he has not explored enough to be sure of his own abilities, and therefore sometimes craves support, reassurance, and control. The result is that one minute he is struggling for freedom and the next he is seeking control. Any parent with an adolescent at home knows that the cues given by the child for support and freedom are not clearly discernible. When the parent thinks the youth wants support he may want freedom, with conflict as the inevitable result. The college community faces this same problem, and it must try to discern the adolescent's needs and measure out freedom and support as they are needed.

As the young adult seeks his own identity he will investigate new ideas and values, explore the world through experience, and relate these experiences to his abilities. He will draw conclusions about the meaning of life, his vocation, his abilities. Subsequently he will commit himself to those ideas and values which are in keeping with the new world-life view as he sees it, and will relate this view to his unique self-concept as it changes and expands. This exploration frequently may cause him to depart from ideas, values, and behavior patterns which his parents have superimposed upon him and which they still expect him to follow. Such a reaction to parental pressures is likely to produce in the student anxiety, fear, a sense of isolation, a feeling of freedom, and—in an evangelical, fundamentalist environment—many guilt feelings.

The student has at least two ways of responding in the face of these inner tensions. One is to regress and return to parental expectations and values; the other is to continue in his individualism and find support and acceptance elsewhere during this period of transition. Without such support only the very strong will not regress and conform to parental pressures, because the lack of support and security will leave him afraid and isolated.

A peer group or an individual on campus often can give the necessary support. Occasionally, a professor can serve as a sympathetic authority figure to help in this period of self-discovery. This professor cannot assume the parental role, but must be a source of support, encouragement, and understanding. This transition period is often traumatic for parents, student, and college, especially if the college assumes a parental role.

One of the most sensitive areas in the personal identity crisis is the student's religious perspective. When a student enters this necessary stage of development, the religious commitments of youth and adolescence are often put into a free-floating state until they can be separated from parental religious views and he can fit them into a more mature picture of himself and his world. If a college assumes a strong parental role in this area, a young person may discard or suspend religious commitments as a by-product of rebellion toward authority figures rather than acting upon mature reflection.

The student knows that religious commitment is the most sensitive area of concern in the homes of most evangelical Christians. When this commitment is questioned or tentatively rejected, it is often the result of independence strivings. In essence the young people are saying: "I've cut the apron strings," "I'm on my own," "I can think for myself now." We should not be overly concerned about this reaction but should try to understand it. The more authoritarian and rigid the home, the more this tactic appears necessary to the developing person. The ideal college will appeal more to the student's mature reflection and less to the rebellious, impulsive, and emotionally loaded religious evaluation. In essence the college should assume less of the parental role in order to be more successful in this area.

The identity crisis as it relates to sex is a problem, especially for college males. There is clinical evidence that men accepted in colleges now have more "feminine" interests than did the students of a decade ago. The reason for this change is that we are getting more males who are closely identified with their mothers because the father's influence frequently is minimal. This identification tends to produce in males characteristics which in our Western culture are classified as "feminine." Such characteristics would be passiveness, artistic interests, domestic interests such as cooking and housekeeping, empathy, sensitivity, and a deeper religious interest. There is a minimum interest in aggressive athletic endeavors, body strength, and competition.

The reasons for this situation are complex but can be ferreted out. For one thing, in our society the fathers have been abdicating their child-rearing responsibilities to the mother. Also, our school systems all the way to high school are geared for the sedate, responsive girls, not for the wiggly, rough-and-tumble boys. Boys who are close to the mother and therefore assume many of her interests and behavior patterns tend to do better in school, where the teacher is usually a woman. Ultimately, boys with this behavior pattern tend to enjoy school more and become better students. When colleges increase academic entrance requirements, they increase the probability of obtaining more males with feminine interests.

From the point of view of abnormal behavior, this situation tends to increase the number of males who are having sex role problems and who may think they are asexual or homosexual. In some cases it tends to produce Don Juans who are out to prove to the world and to themselves that they are virile, adequate males. This problem should be brought to the attention of all interested in higher education.

It is commonly assumed in our American culture that if one is going to succeed in life, he must have a college education. This appears especially true of the male population, but for different reasons it is true of women also. Women need college not primarily for vocational aspirations but for social recognition and to increase the probability of marrying one of these aspiring educated men.

. .In the identity crisis a person must relate his abilities to some form of vocational aspiration. The major problem for most students is that of choosing one of the many vocations possible. The choices seem infinite and the student's under-

122

standing of his abilities or interests is not well developed. Some students come to college with preconceived vocational aspirations which often must undergo revision. The choice of the medical profession is probably one of the most obvious examples. In our society much social prestige is connected with this occupation so that it is natural for many to choose this path. But after the first course in chemistry the student is faced realistically with his ability and interest in science. Often this precipitates the identity crisis experience, and hopefully the student can come into a fruitful period of self-discovery.

Among Christian families in the evangelical subculture, many students go to college with preconceived aspirations toward a church-oriented, religious vocation. In the period of self-evaluation this early vocational commitment must be reevaluated and either confirmed or discarded. This is not easy for the student. Although he may experience a great sense of relief if he changes his vocational plans, he may also have lingering guilt feelings that he has betrayed the will of God. In order to dispel these, he must gain a new view of God's providential care and guidance. A student cannot isolate these early vocational commitments but must include them in the sweeping reevaluation of himself and the world in which he lives.

Perhaps it could be said of the college student in summary that he is not all sugar and spice nor all puppy-dog tails; he is a real person in a struggle to find himself in a complex and often frightening world of ideas, values, and change. He needs someone to listen to him and to try to understand rather than judge him.

BIBLIOGRAPHY

Erikson, Erik. "Identity and the Life Cycle," *Psychological Issues,* Vol. 1, No. 1, 1959.

Jacob, P. E. *Changing Values in College.* New York: Harper & Row, Inc., 1957.

Sanford, N., editor. *The American College.* New York: John Wiley and Son, Inc., 1962.

CONVERSION

Man can be converted to worthy or unworthy causes; he can be victimized by deliberate manipulations. Christians, in an effort to make other men Christian, have sometimes misused this psychological potential to get results.

13

CONVERSION

Manipulation or New Birth?

"I BELIEVE God has led me to say that someone is going to be in an automobile accident tonight and will not have another opportunity to respond to the gospel."

These are the actual words of an evangelist attempting to get a visible response from a group of teenagers at the conclusion of an evangelistic service. This man, claiming to be God's messenger, was trying to influence impressionable young people. Using a spectacular appeal to fear, he tried to move them toward commitment. And he claimed the direction of God's leading. The sincerity of the man's dedication to the cause of Christ is not necessarily questioned, but the technique he used to manipulate teenagers is. This chapter will try to bring into focus some of the psychological implications of the conversion experience for the Christian.

Evangelical Christianity places great importance on a personal religious experience which is usually labeled the "conversion experience," or the "new birth." This existential moment, this leap of faith, this act of personal com-

mitment to God, is the minimum requirement for acceptance into the church of Jesus Christ. The conversion
experience is perceived as the beginning point—a turning
from self-centered concerns toward Christ and his
church—and should progressively culminate in a new orientation, outlook, and behavior pattern which is uniquely
Christian. Some Christians expect to see immediate, dramatic changes in habits, attitudes, and personality characteristics following the conversion experience. They think
that if an alcoholic is converted, he will immediately stop
his drinking. This holds true for other habit patterns such
as swearing, smoking, expressing anger, drug addiction,
gossip or judgmental attitudes. A person who does not
change observably in the prescribed direction is often labeled "insincere," "lacking in faith," and probably "not
truly born again."

Before we can proceed further into a discussion of conversion, we need to ge our definition clear. The psychologist
usually perceives conversion as a lawful, tension-con-
flict experience which tends to reorient a person and is
manifested in many forms of religious, political, and social
behavior. The psychologist does not consider this phenomenon uniquely Christian, although it has obvious manifestations in Christianity. The lawfulness of the phenomenon is
especially important to note.

In his insightful little book entitled *The Christian Life
and the Unconscious,* Ernest White helps us to clarify the
issue from a Christian perspective. It is his suggestion that
we carefully differentiate between *conversion,* which is basically a natural psychological experience, and the *new
birth,* which is the important theological concern for Christianity. It is possible that the new birth and the conversion
experience may occur at the same time; it is also possible
that they may not. A person may be a Christian and never
go through a psychological conversion experience. On the
other hand, a person may have a conversion experience
and not be born again. The great danger arises when one
gives a spiritual interpretation to a psychological phenomenon. To equate an emotional response to a plea with the
working of the Holy Spirit is presumptive and Scripturally
unwarranted. Ernest White suggests that the new birth is

an act of God which has no immediate external manifestations and takes place in the unconscious life of man. This clear distinction between the experience the psychologists call *conversion* and the theological interpretation of God's grace called the *new birth* is very valuable and should help reduce the confusion.

The biographies and autobiographies of men and women throughout the history of the church illustrate the fact that at times the psychological conversion experience and the theological counterpart, the new birth, occur at the same time. Because this is sometimes the case, it is frequently taken as the "model" salvation experience which should be common to all Christians. As a result, many are encouraged to squeeze themselves into this mold whether they fit it or not.

This lawful pattern of the conversion experience looks something like this:

1. Previous secure patterns of living are disrupted by such events as illness, death to loved ones, family relocation, vacations, camps.

2. There is an increase in emotional tension, which may take the form of fear, guilt, sorrow, joy, or compassion.

3. This tension increases to an intense degree, demanding some form of resolution.

4. A possible solution is offered, either verbally or in writing.

5. The person commits himself to the cause directly related to the solution.

6. The by-products of this commitment are a sense of tranquility (inner peace) and an evangelistic fervor for the cause to which the person has committed himself.

7. This evangelistic fervor will slowly diminish, so that the person tends to search for a renewal of his peace of mind and enthusiastic involvement.

8. A person often undergoes subsequent mini-conversions (such as rededication), which have some of the satisfying by-products of the original commitment.

The fact that this sequence of events occurs in the experiences of non-Christians is beyond doubt. William Sargant in his provocative book *Battle for the Mind* cites many examples of political and religious non-Christian conversion which follow this lawful sequence. This is an important point; all Christians should be aware of it because it should influence the mode and content of Christian evangelism.

To point to one's conversion experience and its subsequent by-products as a major apologetic for believing in Christ is inappropriate. The intelligent listener can answer that some Buddhists, Muslims, and converted communists say the same thing. The most that one can say about the conversion experience is that man is so constituted that he can have this experience. But it is not unique to Christianity. A "look what it has done for me" defense for Christianity, whether referring to the conversion experience or to subsequent "Christian" experiences, is a dubious reason for believing in Christ. The fact that the by-products of the conversion experience do not last and have to be reintroduced through subsequent experiences is usually not mentioned in personal evangelism where the personal experience is the main apologetic.

It appears that every psychological by-product of Christianity can be reproduced in almost every religion or ism. Meaning in life, a relief from the burdens of guilt feelings, an awareness of being loved—these are not uniquely Christian. The person weighed down with a burden of guilt feelings may find in Christianity a source of forgiveness. The person searching for something to live and die for may find purpose and meaning the most important psychological element in Christianity. Another person may express deep appreciation for the awareness that he is loved by God and other Christians. Each person will respond differently, but these responses are not unique to Christianity. Other isms and religions can provide purpose in life, relieve guilt feelings, and give a person the awareness of being loved by the committed group. Christianity does not have a corner on these psychological by-products.

Throughout the history of the church, men have ascribed in pragmatic fashion the working of the Holy Spirit to all forms of evangelistic coercion. The death-bed story; the heart-rending story of the deprived child; the appeals to fear, death, hell; the pulsating emotive music; the appeals to all forms of personal inadequacies and incongruities; all

130

have been used and abused in evangelistic efforts to "get results."

I remember hearing an evangelist tell a long, elaborated, colorfully descriptive account of the night his brother-in-law resisted the pleas of the Holy Spirit in an evangelistic service. The evangelist's conclusion was that the Holy Spirit had never returned to convict the man and that night his brother-in-law committed the "unpardonable sin."

Perhaps most coercive evangelistic efforts are not this obvious or extreme, but the list of illustrations can go on and on. Pragmatically, coercive techniques of this type have been used successfully to manipulate people—and they will produce "results"—i.e. some people will respond to the leader's suggestions. With the increased emotional involvement, there is the increased possibility of producing a conversion experience. What this type of manipulation does is to elevate the emotional component in decision making and minimize—in fact sometimes eliminate—the reasoning capacity of man. Such manipulation has been dramatically designated as a "rape of the mind"—a manipulation for personal or group purposes.

Some have suggested that since the new birth sometimes does parallel the psychological conversion, then perhaps the end of high pressure evangelism justifies the means. They say, If it will work, why not use it, since the cause is right and just? I think this argument is inadequate for several reasons.

First, how can we knowingly allow these means to be used for our cause and at the same time condemn others who use them? They can then accuse us of manipulation and coercion.

Also, the person undergoing the experience often becomes confused when the momentary effects wear off and the emotional impact of the moment dissipates. He finds it difficult to make the transition from this mountain-top experience to the valley of everyday living. I would suggest that the dashing to pieces of the sincere hopes of people who have experienced a psychological conversion or mini-conversion is one of the main factors in people's discouragement with Christianity. They often conclude that they have tried to obtain this final state of commitment and ho-

131

liness only to find that the experience did not last. It is often interpreted by them to mean that God just cannot be trusted, or that Christianity does not work.

Another reason, and probably the most important one, is the high value that we should place on man's rational processes and personal integrity. Man is a human being. Each man has his own uniqueness, and if he is to be respected as a person he should not be manipulated like an object, but should be treated with dignity. The objectifying and dehumanizing of man is already one of the major sources of frustration today in our computerized culture.

And finally, what right have we to usurp the role of God's Spirit? We act as if he were impotent and we were forced to do all the work for him. If I understand the Scriptures correctly, we are to present the good news, but only God's Spirit can give a man a new perspective and a new life.

Now all of this does not suggest that emotions are illegitimate and have no rightful place in religious experience. It is to say that a balance of thinking and feeling should be the rule. A person should never be asked to place reason behind emotion, or vice versa. The gospel itself is laden with emotional content which should not be avoided. A presentation of the message of God's redemptive grace will touch man's emotional being, making manipulations by the speaker unnecessary.

Some people are more sensitive to an emotional appeal, with its potential conversion experience, than others. It appears that the following persons are more likely to respond to an emotional appeal and are therefore more likely candidates for a psychological conversion experience.

1. Those who have great capacity to empathize with their fellow men. Such persons are sensitive to people's suffering, to human injustice and privations.

2. Those who have a very sensitive and strong conscience which controls much of their life. These people will be sensitive to appeals which emphasize the incongruities between what they want to be and what they are.

3. Those who are mentally unhealthy. These people tend to be more likely to respond to an appeal which offers an easy solution to their chronic inner discomforts

and tensions. In other words, mentally healthy people are less prone to have emotionally laden conversion experiences.

4. Those who are looking for external controls and stability. These people are likely subjects. This is especially true of adolescents who are apprehensive about leaving the support of the home and venturing out by themselves. They are looking for a source of stability to replace the parents.

5. Those who are sensitive to the aesthetic qualities of life such as art, music, nature, etc. They respond to the world with their emotions and are more likely to become involved than those who tend to critically and objectively analyze the world around them.

6. Those with less education. They are likely candidates because they are less able to perceive the accuracy of a presentation.

7. Those who have been taught to expect an emotional conversion experience. These people are more likely to have one.

Some individuals have insulated themselves from their emotions for various reasons and are almost impossible to penetrate by an emotional appeal. This has been interpreted by some as resistance to the Holy Spirit. If one equates an emotional response with the work of the Holy Spirit, then one might find this conclusion logical. Since this equation is not the case, then Christianity must understand this man and should not interpret the veracity of his Christian persuasion by overt responses to an emotive appeal.

You may ask, then, "What is unique about Christianity if the conversion experience is not?" The difference is the content. The Communist commits himself to communism, the Muslim to Allah, and the Christian to Christ. The truth of each must rest on criteria other than experience. The Christian must rest ultimately on the historicity of the life, death, and resurrection of Jesus. Did he rise from the dead or not? It is at this point, and this point alone, that the Christian defense must be made. If Christ rose from the dead then what he had to say and what he did is of great significance; but if he did not rise from the dead, then let us identify with Paul's reaction when he said, "Let us rather eat, drink, and be merry for tomorrow we die" (I Corinthians 15:32). A person should be confronted primarily with Jesus Christ and his death and resurrection, not with personal experience.

But what about the work of the Holy Spirit? The Bible claims that no man can call Christ "Lord" unless the Holy Spirit reveals it. This is a theological statement and has no observable counterpart in human behavior. From a theological point of view we state that the things of Christ are foolishness to mankind until the Holy Spirit makes them relevant. As I understand the position of orthodox Christianity, the work of the Holy Spirit is to reveal Christ through the Word of God. As man is confronted with the Word read, the Word preached, and the Word sung, the Spirit of God illuminates and applies the Word to the life of man. In the new birth man is confronted with Christ through the Word, and he responds to Christ as the Holy Spirit makes the truth of the Word relevant. How God's Spirit unites with man's physiological and psychological interactions is a mystery which we probably never will solve because there appears to be no psychological counterpart to this illuminating spiritual dimension.

To the Christian psychologist the conversion phenomenon is interesting, as is any other investigation of human behavior. Like most of man's behavior, it points to the fact that we are wonderfully made and very complex. The fact that man can undergo an experience which can reorient him, which can give him purpose in life, and can change his behavior is wonderful indeed; and the Christian can give God praise because this is a potential in His creation.

Man can be converted to worthy or unworthy causes; he can be victimized by deliberate manipulations. Christians, in an effort to make other men Christian, have sometimes misused this psychological potential to get results. In such manipulations it would appear that we want to perform the work of the Holy Spirit and coerce man to capitulate to the claims of Christ. Christ still claims today that if he is lifted up he will draw all men to himself. This claim says nothing about *how* he will do it. But it is his work, not ours.

134

BIBLIOGRAPHY

Sargant, William. *Battle for the Mind*. New York: Doubleday and Company, Inc., 1957.

White, Ernest. *The Christian Life and the Unconscious*. New York: Harper & Row, Inc., 1955.

YES! BUT TO WHAT?

"I wish I could believe like I did when I was a child."
This desire to regress to an earlier form of behavior is
understandable but impossible.

14.

YES! BUT TO WHAT?

In portraying Yurii Zhivago in his famous book *Dr. Zhivago*, Boris Pasternak places his literary fingers on the pulse of one of man's basic dilemmas—the need to have something to live for. After Yurii had sent his beloved Lara away, knowing that it was the last time he would see her, he began the path of psychological and physical deterioration which often takes place when man has no longer any reason to live. Understanding the problem of meaning in life is crucial to our understanding of man, because the search for meaning motivates much of what he does and the way he does it.

That man has a basic need to find meaning and purpose in life is an assumption made by existentialists about the nature of man. If he can accept this assumption, the psychologist's task is to investigate in the laboratory and in psychotherapy the way this need is expressed in the everyday affairs of living. It is reasonable to suggest that meaning and purpose in life are expressed in the various forms of commitments which men make—to a person, a goal, a movement, or a combination of these.

A college student once shared with me some of his anxieties and problems. One was meaninglessness in life and lack of commitment, and his desire for both. He had been brought up in a Christian home and was always involved in church activities. As he matured he found his budding faith and Christian experience personally meaningful, and it was a continued source of strength for him throughout his early adolescent years. Then he went to college, where he was confronted with new ways of looking at man, people with different types of Christian experience from his, and new interpretations of Scripture. He began to see the world in broader perspective as he pursued studies in the humanities and the social sciences. His discovery that men were *very* complex challenged the simplified "Biblical" view of man he had been taught in his youth. He discovered that there were few "black and whites" in the area of personal values, and that men must be understood in light of their individual experiences and social contexts. He found that there were many questions and few answers—something which his home and church did not accept or understand.

As he reviewed his past experiences in light of these new insights, he saw that many of his "Christian" experiences were really self-deceptive, often the result of parental or evangelistic coercion which appealed to his very unstable adolescent emotions. He discovered that some of the rules for Christian living presented to him were perhaps effective for some people but not for him. He was disturbed, and a little angered, that he had been manipulated by various forms of direct and indirect pressure. He had never found a form of Christian experience which was uniquely his, though he accepted the basic tenets of Christianity. Because he had often been deceived during these formative years, he began to question the validity of his earlier experiences. Since he now saw life as complex, he challenged anything which seemed to give simple, easy answers; therefore, the "simple" theology which he had been presented in youth became suspect.

This sincere questioning left him with an attitude of caution and skepticism regarding his religious experience and much of Christian doctrine. There was now an emotional void which once had been filled with his immature commitment to Christ and His church. Though much of his evaluation of his past was probably accurate, this did not meet his affective need for present commitment. He stated his dilemma to me like this: "I wish I could believe like I did when I was a child." His desire to regress to an earlier form of behavior was understandable, but impossible. A regression of this type would not be satisfying for any period of time and eventually would only increase his inner conflicts. He will have to find a commitment, hopefully a Christian one, which will fit into his more mature world.

This case exemplifies the universal need of man to commit himself to something, to make life meaningful and worthwhile. What will this student do to fill the void? He, like all men, has many options open to him.

He may avoid facing the vacuum by running from the haunting questions which will lead to personal involvement. This would entail rushing headlong into all forms of activities to keep from the solitude in which these significant questions of existence are conceived and break through into consciousness. He might lose himself in active or vicarious enjoyment of athletics, either watching or playing sports of all kinds. Many find a brief reprieve from the deep questions of life on the golf course or by watching the variety of athletic displays on television. A woman may lose herself in a series of coffee chats, cocktail parties, telephone conversations, or school and political activities, ending the day in exhaustion with no time or energy to ask significant questions about life and death.

Others may fill this void with various definite commitments. People can live for their children, but those who do live in continual fear that their children will be taken from them through some tragic event. They would then be left not only with the natural sorrow that such a loss produces, but without purpose in life. Some may commit themselves to the cause of science with its many challenges and facets of research. Some may chase the illusive goal of fame, living for promotion and recognition. For those who so strive, it is a major personal catastrophe if they are passed over and eliminated from consideration for promotion. They must reevaluate and change their reason for living lest depression and despair continually overwhelm them.

One of the obvious forms of commitment is to a political

141

or social cause. William Sargant's *Battle for the Mind* is an interesting and provocative book in the field of psychology and conversion. The author describes the "psychological conversion" of Arthur Koestler, who under the pressures of guilt feelings, discouragements, and failure committed himself to the cause of communism. The by-products of this commitment were a sense of peace, a zeal to tell others of this great cause, and a sense of purpose in life. It is likely that people who have committed themselves to social reform movements of various types find this vacuum of purposelessness filled.

There are many other worthy and unworthy causes to which a man may commit himself in an attempt to fill this ever-present need. In my profession I know of many who have committed themselves to a particular theory of personality, in essence a philosophy of life; or to science, with the hope that it will usher in a "new world." Such commitments will, they hope, help pacify the inevitable, internal gnawing need for purposefulness and meaning to existence. Still others have committed themselves to art, music, sensualism of all descriptions, or the "pursuit of knowledge."

This need for purpose must be met either by repression, active avoidance, or some form of commitment. What will happen to this student referred to earlier? How will he fill the void? Will he commit himself to some social cause which reflects Christian morality, or will he lose himself in a series of sensual experiences to avoid the issue? Perhaps he will commit himself to the pursuit of "truth" through art or philosophy, or throw himself into "spiritualism" with its emotional reassurances. He could, of course, regress and try to fit his more mature faith into his immature religious experiences of youth. Perhaps he will be able to find a psychologically satisfying answer in a combination of these— or in some other commitment.

What about his commitment to Christ and His church? Ultimately, it is hoped, he will find commitment to God and His church a vital part of his life. But we must not give the impression that this commitment is easy or that there are ready-made formulas to produce it automatically. Commitment to Christ cannot be forced, but it is obvious that man has met God in dynamic encounter throughout history, and that occasionally this meeting occurs in the strangest ways and most unexpected places. It is also true that we are confronted with the repeated command of God through His Word: "Commit your way to the Lord."

God has made man in such a way that he must commit himself to something to attain an inner sense of well-being. God's plan is that man should commit himself to God and thereby have a reason to live and a dynamic which gives purpose to every experience. It is the hope of every Christian that every man will find in Christ the answer to this ever-present need.